PENNSYLVANIA STATION
OF
P. T. & T. R. R
FEB. 18TH 1910

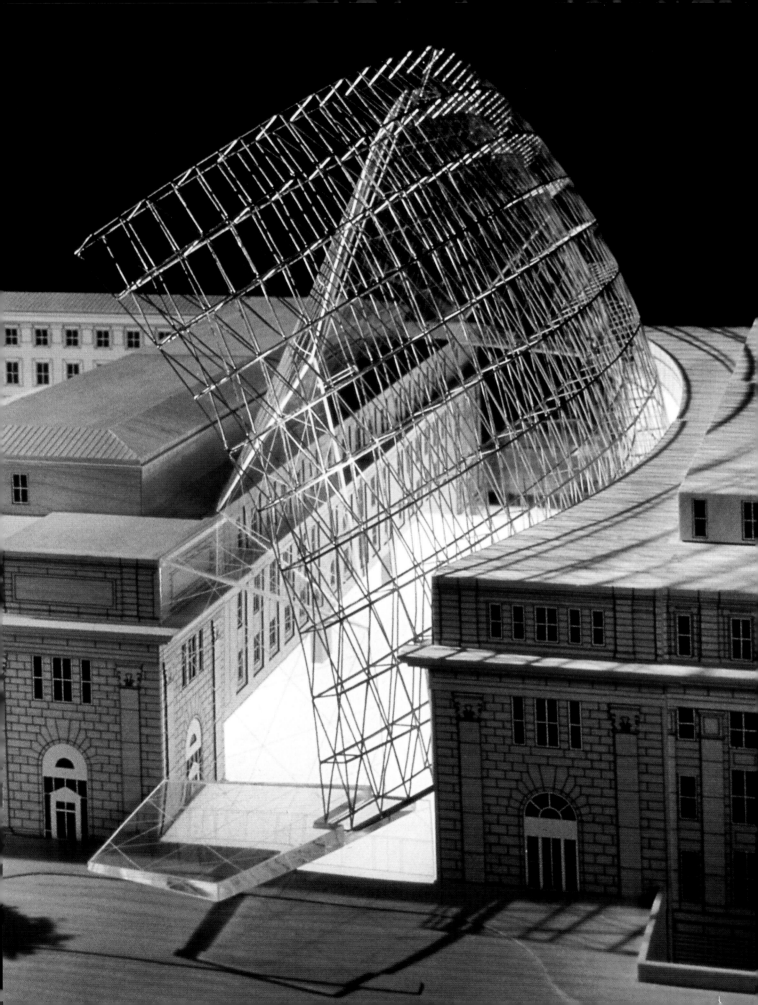

New York's Pennsylvania Stations

HILARY BALLON

with a photo essay by Norman McGrath

and a contribution by Marilyn Jordan Taylor,

Skidmore, Owings & Merrill

 W. W. NORTON & COMPANY   NEW YORK · LONDON

For information about permission to reproduce selections from this book, write to
Permissions, W. W. Norton & Company, Inc., 500 Fifth Avenue, New York, NY 10110

The text of this book is composed in Monotype Garamond and FF Eureka Sans
with display set in FF Din Light
Manufacturing by Colorprint Offset, Hong Kong
Book design and composition by Kristina Kachele
Production manager: Leeann Graham

Library of Congress Cataloging-in-Publication Data

Ballon, Hilary.
New York's Pennsylvania Stations / Hilary Ballon ; with a photographic
essay by Norman McGrath and a contribution by Marilyn Jordan Taylor.
p. cm.
Includes bibliographical references and index.
ISBN 0-393-73078-6
1. Pennsylvania Station (New York, N.Y.). 2. Railroad stations—New York
(State)—New York. 3. Historic buildings—New York (State)—New York.
I. McGrath, Norman. II. Title.

TF302.N7 B35 2002
385.3'14'0974710dc21
2001044232

W. W. Norton & Company, Inc., 500 Fifth Avenue New York, N.Y. 10110
www.wwnorton.com
W. W. Norton & Company Ltd., Castle House, 75/76 Wells Street, London W1T 3QT
0 9 8 7 6 5 4 3 2 1

Contents

Acknowledgments, 11

PART 1

The First Pennsylvania Station
by Hilary Ballon, 17

PART 2

A Landmark Dismantled: A Photographic Essay
by Norman McGrath, 109

PART 3

The New Pennsylvania Station
by Marilyn Jordan Taylor, 151

Notes, 197

Select Bibliography, 213

Photography Credits, 215

Index, 217

Acknowledgments

I stand with many writers awed by the majesty of the first Pennsylvania Station and the boldness of the underlying civil engineering program. I came to know the building through books. Two in particular set me going: Lorraine Diehl's *The Late, Great Pennsylvania Station*, which introduces a riveting architectural story, and Carl Condit's outstanding two-volume study, *The Port of New York*, which addresses the infrastructure of rail transportation in and about New York City. This book takes the story of Pennsylvania Station up to the present; it covers the original building, its demolition, and the new station now under construction. The full story could not have been told without the contributions of Norman McGrath, whose demolition photographs are published here for the first time, and of Marilyn Jordan Taylor, chair at Skidmore, Owings & Merrill. Permission to publish the designs of SOM was granted by the Pennsylvania Station Development Corporation. I am grateful to Michael Royce, John Gerber, and Marijke Smit as well as to past president Alexandros E. Washburn who encouraged this project from the outset. I salute their passion for Pennsylvania Station, extensive knowledge of its history, and dedication to the new station they are bringing to life despite awesome hurdles. At Skidmore, Owings & Merrill, my thanks go to Dionne Gadsden Cobb and Michael Fei, who graciously fielded my questions and assembled visual materials.

My own essay focuses on the urban design of the first Pennsylvania Station. Although long recognized as a masterpiece of Charles McKim, Pennsylvania Station has been more celebrated than analyzed. The interpretation offered here takes issue with the prevailing view of the station as a nostalgic dream of ancient Rome. It shifts attention to the modern functions of the station and to McKim's ambitious effort to reconcile ancient and modern building arts. The essay also addresses the real estate activities of the Pennsylvania Railroad around the station in order to understand the lackluster development in this neighborhood relative to the vigorous urbanism around Grand Central Terminal.

My account relies on the archives of McKim, Mead & White and of the Pennsylvania Railroad. The McKim, Mead & White material is located in the New-York Historical Society, where Holly Hinman assisted my research efforts, and in the Avery Architectural and Fine Arts Library at Columbia University, which I am lucky to call home. The series of construction photographs by Louis Dreyer reproduced in this book come from Avery Library, and it gives me special pleasure to feature this treasure as well as other photographs under the guardianship of Angela Giral at Avery Library, who granted permission to publish the material. I would especially like to thank Claudia Funke, curator of rare books, and Janet Parks, curator of archives and drawings, for their counsel, respect for the mission of scholarly research, and the reasonable way they balance the competing needs to protect Avery's rich resources and to share it with a wider audience.

Although other kinds of historians have preceded me, this is the first time an art historian has mined the vast archives of the Pennsylvania Railroad for material on the station. The archives of the Pennsylvania Railroad are divided among three libraries: the Hagley Museum and Library, the New York Public Library, and the Pennsylvania State Archives. The harvest was especially rich in the Hagley Museum and Library, which has, among other things, the papers of Samuel Rea, the man in charge of the New York building program. My cicerone in all matters relating to the Pennsy (the nickname of the Pennsylvania Railroad Company) was Christopher Baer, curator at the Hagley, to whom I am indebted. The Hagley Library is a scholar's dream, not least because Chris Baer superbly organized and indexed the Pennsy archives. My research was partially funded by a grant-in-aid from the Hagley Museum.

Arif Turkeli shared his expertise about the Pennsylvania Railroad, read an early version of this text, which he helped to improve, and made available his extensive collection of postcards, some of which are reproduced in the book. Ellen Belcher, formerly curator of special collections at Long Island University, alerted me to the spectacular construction photographs of the Hudson River tunnels in her care. I am grateful to her as well as to Eileen Morales at the Museum of the City of New York for assisting my research.

This book emerged from an exhibition I curated at the Miriam and Ira D. Wallach Art Gallery, Columbia University, in 2000, and was coordinated with an undergraduate seminar I taught on McKim, Mead & White. The collaboration of Sarah Weiner, director of the Wallach Art Gallery, and Jeanette Silverthorne, assistant director, was invaluable. The students in my seminar created what was, at least for me, a memorable learning experience. This book arises from the critical synergy between teaching and research that Columbia University nurtures.

Finally, this book would not exist if not for Nancy Green, an editor who somehow finds a way to meet the demands of commercial book publishing while valuing original scholarship.

Two personal convictions inform this book. The first is that the past bears on the present in meaningful ways. The second is the importance of public architecture; it improves the quality of urban life, transforms utility into art, and shapes the identity of our communities. Public architecture is a neglected but vital ingredient in our lives as citizens.

My essay is dedicated to my beloved children, Sophie and Charles Kramer, angels and engaged citizens in the making.

New York's Pennsylvania Stations

Part 1

The First Pennsylvania Station

Hilary Ballon

Pennsylvania Station was unnecessary.

The train tracks were four stories underground. Nothing above street level was needed for railroad operations. Functional requirements could have been met by covered entrances to the lower depths, like those to the subway. In short, a big station above ground was superfluous. From a real estate perspective, the optimal solution was to bury the station and build a skyscraper above it since rental income from the tower could finance the station's operating expenses. This approach was adopted at a contemporary railroad station downtown, the Hudson Terminal Buildings (1907–9), where four towers were stacked above a subterranean terminal. At street level, those towers appeared no different than the neighboring skyscrapers of Wall Street; the Hudson Terminal Buildings managed to conceal its special role in sheltering a transportation hub in the basement. The same conditions prevailed with the successor buildings on the site, the World Trade Center that sat above the renamed PATH station. This economic solution had a consequence, however, that was unacceptable to the Pennsylvania Railroad Company: it meant that the station would be invisible from the street.

The Pennsylvania Railroad wanted maximum visibility, so it built a monument covering eight acres, the largest structure of its kind in the world, with a room that dwarfed City Hall and massive granite columns designed not just to endure but also to convey a message of stability and permanence.

The station was a monument to the Pennsylvania Railroad Company's corporate power and financial resources, a symbol befitting one of the world's richest and best-run corporations—a corporation capable of civil engineering projects on a mammoth scale and sufficiently well endowed to forsake a potentially lucrative skyscraper in order to build a landmark. Yet in a remarkable conversion of public perceptions, Penn Station transcended its corporate identity. A creation of private enterprise, it assumed the standing of a public structure, in part because it played a fundamental role in the life of New York City, in part because its grand architecture enabled the station to embody civic hopes and values.

One value was unrestricted access and movement. Penn Station celebrated the importance of transportation to the city. "In no better way can the City be developed," a leader of the Pennsylvania Railroad reflected in 1910, "than in connection with the transportation companies in properly caring for the arrival and departure of travelers."[1] The rail lines nourished the city. They enabled New York City to thrive and grow by giving millions of people the essential ability to cross considerable distances with speed and comfort. Unimpeded circulation in the metropolitan region was possible only after the railroad conquered a number of geological, technological, and engineering hurdles: the ability to overcome rivers, silt, and bedrock; to harness electricity to power trains; and to build tunnels underwater. Penn Station was the capstone of an underground chain of tunnels that stretched from New Jersey across Manhattan to Queens. Where the encircling arms of the Hudson and East Rivers once isolated Manhattan, now steel threads of track bound the city to the continent. The Pennsylvania project changed the law of nature; it annihilated the water barrier and reshaped the landscape of New York into a continuous network of rail connections.

That engineering achievement was honored at the very heart of the building, in the concourse where passengers witnessed the linear ballet of moving trains. No smoke, no need for open-air ventilation in the new age of electrification, hence the concourse was a fully enclosed, underground space. The canopy of glazed vaults draped the sunken tracks with light and brought sky and earth together. Opposite elements converged in the concourse—sky and earth, stone and steel. The real purpose of this wondrous space was to celebrate unimpeded movement and to observe the seemingly natural flow of trains. The granite walls evoked stability, but the station was really all about motion.

Another value embodied in the station was the importance of the city. Penn Station was an homage to New York, a testimony to its status as the commercial capital of the world. No other city would have justified the railroad's huge capital investment or merited a building of such colossal scale. The station was a colossal achievement in all senses: size, expense, quality of design, and scope. Penn Station was designed to accommodate half a million people daily, and to sort and process the traffic of a miniature city. It was designed to dignify a routine aspect of modern life and to reflect the station's central and dynamic role in the city. Finally, the station was designed to endure, like the monuments of ancient Rome it emulated. No wonder that in 1912 the head of Columbia University's School of Architecture ranked Penn Station as one of the seven wonders of the modern world. "People will admire it for centuries to come. . . . [It is] among the few buildings in this city that are constructed with sufficient solidity to last for several centuries."[2] The monumentality of Penn Station was a measure of the power and ambition of New York City, a sign of its historic destiny.

But the marvel stood for little more than a half-century. No less than its creation, the demolition of Penn Station in the 1960s was symptomatic of New York City—its commercial ethos, serene detachment from the past, and wanton disregard of the civic sphere. Demolition sadly proved that the great superstructure was unnecessary; the railroad continued to operate in underground facilities. But as sometimes happens with a major loss, it awakened New Yorkers to the value of the first Pennsylvania Station and the ennobling respect accorded its users. The station embodied a humane idea that was, and still is, essential to the life of New York.

THE PROBLEM

The Pennsylvania Railroad could not reach Manhattan. Since 1871, when the Pennsylvania Railroad Company acquired the United Railroads of New Jersey, the line terminated at Jersey City, on the Jersey shore of the Hudson River. Passengers were obliged to disembark from trains, baggage in tow, and cross the Hudson River by ferry to docks in lower Manhattan (Figs. 1.1 and 1.2).[3] The ferries that crisscrossed the Hudson as well as the East River were an insistent reminder that Manhattan was an island and accessible almost exclusively by boat; in 1900 the Brooklyn Bridge was the only span across the rivers. The nineteenth century had undergone a transportation revolution, from horsepower to steampower to electric traction, yet the ferries plying New York harbor remained a constant. Of course, ferry ships also improved over the century but, compared to train travel and the amenities it offered, the ferry was a holdover from the past.[4] The ride was uncomfortable, hazardous, vulnerable to weather, and slow—especially relative to the ever greater levels of passenger comfort, reliability, and speed achieved by the railroads.

The railroads had steadily reduced travel time over the course of the nineteenth century. In 1839, when the first long-distance run between Philadelphia and Jersey City was introduced, the trip took four and a half hours. In 1902, the Pennsylvania Railroad made

Pennsylvania Railroad Depot.   Jersey City, N. J.

The West Street and North River Piers,
New York City.

1.1. Pennsylvania Station and
Ferry Terminal, Jersey City,
New Jersey.

1.2. The ferry terminal of
the Pennsylvania Railroad at
Cortlandt Street, New York City.

the trip in 79 minutes—more than three times faster.[5] The two great rival train systems in the metropolitan region, the Pennsylvania and the New York Central, were competing for speed records at the turn of the century. As a result, the distance from New York to Chicago, Washington, and Florida was shrinking, as measured in travel time. But the mile across the Hudson didn't shrink; if anything, it seemed to expand because the railroad had awakened and fostered an appetite for speed and efficiency that the ferry could not satisfy. Trains could get travelers to Jersey City from virtually any major city at average speeds of 40 to 80 miles per hour. The last mile across the Hudson took twenty minutes in good weather, twice as long when the weather was poor—a snail's pace.

For railroad companies, passenger inconvenience was not the main problem; the river presented a financial problem. The business of railroading, whether moving passengers or freight, depended on the continuous flow of traffic. More traffic meant more ticket sales and higher operating revenues. When passengers experienced slow trains, schedule delays, or difficult transfers, these constrictions of movement translated into lost revenues. The Pennsylvania Railroad made huge investments in rights of way and rolling stock, bridges and viaducts, automatic signals, switching, and motive power precisely to achieve free-flowing, unrestricted movement. By 1900 it had cleared most hurdles on the main lines connecting New York City with Philadelphia, Baltimore, and Washington, and with points west from Pittsburgh to Chicago. Only one major hurdle remained, the Hudson River—a hurdle more important than any other because it restricted access to Manhattan, the commercial capital of the United States.

The explosive growth of New York City at the turn of the century exacerbated the Hudson River bottleneck. In 1896, 94 million New York–bound passengers disembarked from trains at Jersey City. In 1906 the number reached 140 million.[6] New York City was first and foremost a great port and harbor; the Hudson River was its commercial lifeline. Heavy traffic from ocean-bound steamships, freighters, and fleets of ferries operated by six different railroad companies was choking the river and threatening to curtail economic development. The railroad had to find a way to build rails across the Hudson.

The Pennsylvania Railroad's options were analyzed in 1892 in a report prepared by Samuel Rea (1855–1929), special assistant to the president and quintessential railroad man, expert in all technical matters.[7] Equipped with administrative skill as well, Rea was later put in charge of the New York extension and, after rising through the highest executive positions, served as the ninth president of the Pennsylvania Railroad (1913–25). Rea was the Pennsylvania's expert on railroad electrification, the technology which though still in its infancy promised to transform the industry. If any man could look into the future and evaluate the railroad's options, it was Samuel Rea. But in 1892 the future was not at all clear to Rea. The most striking feature of his report was the wide range of options it entertained and the absence of an obvious solution. The railroad was unresolved about the most fundamental choices involved in a New York extension: how to cross the river, by bridge or tunnel; whether to use heavy-weight, long-distance trains or lighter, rapid-transit ones; at what point to cross the river and where to build a station; even whether a Manhattan terminal was necessary at all. Not one of the five potential solutions Rea outlined corresponded with the ultimate plan; none was even close.

The first scheme called for extending the New York City subway system from Manhattan to Jersey City, a solution that eliminated the need for a Pennsylvania terminal in New York City. This proposal was modeled on the City and South London Railway in London, the world's first electric subway which had opened in 1890 and which Rea had traveled to London to see. Another scheme called for completion (and expansion) of a partially constructed Hudson River tunnel with a terminal near Washington Square. A railroad engineer named DeWitt Clinton Haskin had initiated the tunnel in 1873, but the project was abandoned after a blowout in 1880 killed many workers. By 1892 there was evidence that underwater tunnels could be built safely, but tunnels required the railroad to adopt a new form of motive power. Steam engines vomited clouds of smoke and hot cinders that required ventilation in the open air. They could not operate in the enclosed space of a long-run tunnel; even in a short-run tunnel, the risk of fire and asphyxiation posed a serious danger.[8] Rea, therefore, proposed detaching steam engines in New Jersey and hauling cable cars through the Hudson River tunnels. The third scheme, which eschewed the use of rails, did not fundamentally solve the problem. It was to run trains onto ferries and discharge passengers at Eleventh Avenue and 42nd Street for connections with the elevated line.

The fourth scheme involved a circuitous route through the outlying boroughs to a terminal on the East Side of Manhattan. The trains would run from New Jersey across Staten Island and over to Brooklyn by a combination of bridges and tunnels. In Brooklyn the Pennsylvania trains would run along the line of the Long Island Railroad to its terminus in Long Island City, Queens. At that point, Manhattan-bound trains would cross the East River by bridge to a station on Madison Avenue between 37th and 38th Streets, and trains headed for New England would take a bridge over the Hell Gate, a hazardous channel of the East River, to join the New Haven line in the Bronx. Although this solution could not have been viable given its length, complexity, and cost, the Pennsylvania leadership recognized two elements that were essential for its future growth: access to the Long Island Railroad's facilities in Queens and to the New Haven line in the Bronx.

The fifth possible solution to the New York problem was a bridge over the Hudson River leading to a passenger station near Madison Square. Rea's endorsement of the bridge was significant because in 1889, as chief engineer of the B & O's Baltimore belt line, he had solved a railroad problem by building a short-run tunnel for electrified trains. Clearly Rea did not believe the technology was in place in 1892 to build a tunnel through the silt of the Hudson River or to use electric traction on the scale required for New York City.

The Hudson River bridge Rea backed was designed and promoted by Gustav Lindenthal, then a young engineer whose famous bridges — the Manhattan (1909), the

Queensboro (1909), and the Hell Gate (1917)—lay decades in the future. Inspired by the opening of the Brooklyn Bridge in 1883, Lindenthal proposed in 1885 a gargantuan suspension bridge, twice the span of the Brooklyn Bridge (Fig. 1.3).[9] He revised the design over the next few years, in part to convince the Army Corps of Engineers that the North River Bridge, as it was called, would not impede navigation, and in 1890 he obtained a federal charter to build a triple-deck bridge, with fourteen tracks for steam and rapid-transit trains. Although the railroad industry was marked by fierce competition, the paramount importance of traffic flow occasionally led them to cooperate in linking their roads and creating a physically integrated network. Thus bridges were often joint under-takings of two or more roads. Given the high cost of Lindenthal's project, estimated at up to $100 million, he envisioned that the various railroad companies with railheads on the west shore of the Hudson would share the cost of the bridge as well as that of a union (shared) station in Manhattan.[10] In fact, the federal charter barred exclusive use of the bridge by one railroad. Accordingly the scheme collapsed when the smaller companies chose not to participate. The failure of Lindenthal's proposal is usually attributed to its high cost, but this factor is overstated in view of the fact that the Pennsylvania Railroad spent significantly more on its New York extension a decade later. More to the point, the Pennsylvania Railroad was not yet willing in the 1890s to assume the full cost of build-ing a New York extension on its own.

1.3. Project for the North River Bridge by Gustav Lindenthal, 1885.

Decisive action required both a bold leader and technological advancement. The bold leader arrived in June 1899 when Alexander Cassatt (1839–1906) was elected president of the Pennsylvania Railroad. Cassatt was determined to connect the Pennsylvania Railroad to Manhattan and beyond to New England lines, to form the critical remaining link in an otherwise uninterrupted chain running the length of the eastern seaboard and into the Midwest. Toward this end, he bought control of the Long Island Railroad in May 1900. The fit may not have been perfect since the Pennsylvania Railroad was a long-distance carrier and the Long Island Railroad a suburban line—a tension that would eventually play out in Penn Station. But the LIRR's facilities in Brooklyn and Queens were useful, as Rea's report had suggested, for the projected New York extension. Moreover, the Pennsylvania's purchase eliminated the threat of the LIRR connecting with Grand Central Station.

The other precondition was technological readiness, in particular the ability to use electric motive power on the heavy-duty, multicar trains of the Pennsylvania Railroad.[11] Cassatt realized that this condition was met when he attended the opening of the Gare d'Orsay in Paris in the summer of 1900 and witnessed electrically powered trains enter the historic city center through underground tunnels. The New York solution became apparent to Cassatt and Rea. Over the next sixteen months, they plotted the Pennsylvania's entrance into Manhattan and set the railroad on a capital program of unprecedented scale.

Cassatt announced the plan for the Pennsylvania Tunnel Extension and Terminal Project, as it was officially called, in December 1901, and put Rea in charge.[12] It was a civil engineering program of breathtaking ambition and expense. The far-reaching network of tracks and tunnels comprised the following eight components (Fig. 1.4): a transfer station, known as Manhattan Transfer, located at Harrison, New Jersey (near Newark) where steam locomotives were exchanged for electric ones (and vice versa for south-bound trains); a spur line running north from the transfer station across the Hackensack Meadowlands to Weehawken, New Jersey, which was in line with the station site; twin tunnels, each containing one track, descending first through land (Bergen Hill) and continuing under the Hudson River to portals at Tenth Avenue and 32nd Street; the Manhattan railyard and station; two cross-town tunnels in Manhattan, each containing two tracks, under 32nd and 33rd Streets; four tunnels under the East River to Long Island City; the world's largest railyard in Sunnyside, Queens, covering 208 acres, where the Pennsylvania's trains were serviced and turned around; and the most important component, the one which made the extension possible, electrification of the thirteen miles of line between Manhattan Transfer and Sunnyside Yard.[13]

In 1906, Cassatt added another piece to the building program: construction of the New York Connecting Railroad from Sunnyside Yard to Port Morris in the Bronx for connection with the New Haven line. The New York Connecting Railroad, which included the Hell Gate Bridge, was a joint company half owned by the Pennsylvania and the New York, New Haven and Hartford Railroads. Construction started in 1912, soon after Penn Station was completed. Lindenthal's Hell Gate Bridge and the new line were put in service in 1917, extending the Pennsylvania system to New England.[14]

The cost of the New York extension (not including the New York Connecting Railroad) was $113 million, "a greater expenditure than was ever before incurred by a private corporation for a single undertaking," the company proudly acknowledged.[15] Press reports equated it with the Panama Canal for its breadth of vision, scale, and complexity; excavation for the station was dubbed New York's Culebra Cut, after the major excavation through the continental divide.[16] (Alfred Noble, the engineer in charge of the East River tunnels, took a leave of absence in March 1907 to advise the U.S. government on the Panama Canal.) These two vast engineering projects came to embody American ingenuity and power in the early years of the twentieth century.

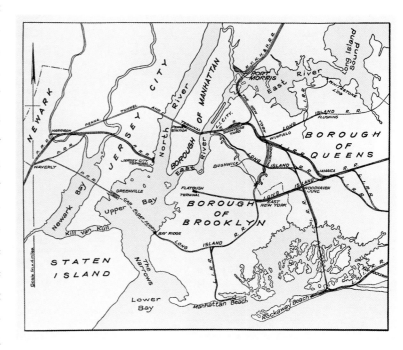

1.4. Map of the New York Extension of the Pennsylvania Railroad Company and the New York Connecting Railroad.

Yet unlike the Panama Canal which was built and financed by the U.S. government, the New York extension was a private venture of the Pennsylvania Railroad. The tunnels, tracks, and monumental station—a huge investment in the infrastructure of New York—were built without public funding, an unimaginable situation today. The city's willingness to close 32nd Street between Seventh and Tenth Avenues and to transfer ownership of a public street to a private corporation for a relatively low price constituted the only form of municipal subsidy the railroad received. The New York extension was "an act of good citizenship," the *Railway Age Gazette* commented, and "a contribution toward the common welfare and toward progress."[17]

The industry magazine failed to mention either the company's profit motive or its

K 24. P. R. R. Tunnels, N. R. D. Section K. (Bergen Hill Tunnels,) from Hackensack Portal, North Cut and Cover Section, and Portal looking East from Sta. 323 + 85.   Dec. 8, 05.

1.5. Bergen Hill Tunnels during construction, December 8, 1905. Photograph by the O'Rourke Engineering Construction Company.

enormous financial resources. In 1902, when the extension was launched, the gross revenues of the Pennsylvania Railroad were slightly under $113 million, and passenger and freight traffic were increasing rapidly every year. The company could comfortably finance the building program.[18]

Of all phases of construction, which lasted from 1903 to 1910, none captured the public imagination more than the death-defying marvel of building tunnels underwater, a feat made possible by the shield method of construction. The shield was essentially a steel sleeve in which the tunnel was constructed. Diggers, using hydraulic jacks, pushed the shield forward, allowing the silt of the riverbed to ooze through a window in the shield. As the shield advanced, rings of cast iron were bolted together inside, and with each new ring, the tunnel was resurveyed. Adjustments were then made to ensure that when the two ends of the tunnel met midway beneath the river, they were aligned. The measure of

K 43. P. R. R. Tunnels, N. R. D. Sect. K. (Bergern Hill
Tunnels,) Hackensack Portal and Approach, looking
East from near Sta. 326+40.   March 8, 06.

their success is impressive: the Hudson tunnels deviated by only ¾ inch in grade and ⅛ inch in horizontal alignment. To judge from the extensive press coverage of tunnel building, the public was fascinated by the crusade underwater by brave sandhogs recruited from around the world.[19] Figures 1.5–1.7 and 1.10–1.13, which have never before been published, come from the files of the O'Rourke Engineering Construction Company, which was the contractor for the North (or Hudson) River Tunnels. Despite changes above ground, these same tunnels are used virtually unchanged to this day.[20]

It is not wrong to see Pennsylvania Station as a glamorous capstone to a more extensive infrastructural improvement, one that was largely underground and invisible but that changed the daily lives of millions of people. Yet to diminish the relative importance of the building would be misleading, for the purpose of the tunnels and the electrification of the lines was in order to have a station in Manhattan. As a railroad expert at the time

1.6. Portals of the Bergen Hill Tunnels in Hackensack, N.J. during construction, March 8, 1906. Photograph by the O'Rourke Engineering Construction Company.

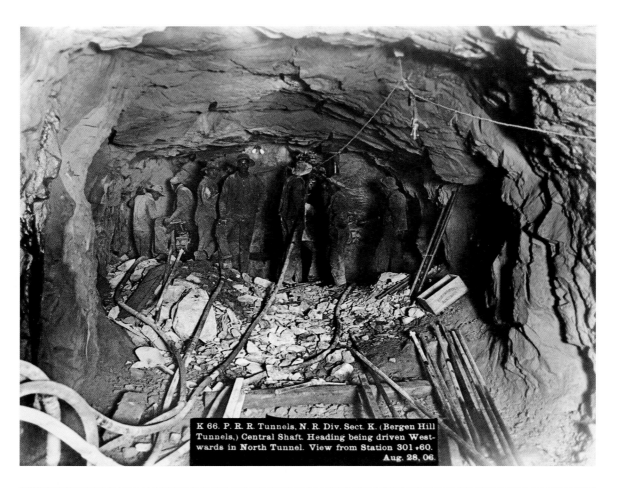

K 66. P. R. R. Tunnels, N. R. Div. Sect. K. (Bergen Hill Tunnels,) Central Shaft. Heading being driven Westwards in North Tunnel. View from Station 301+60.
Aug. 28, 06.

T 49. P. R. R. Tunnels, N. R. Div. River Tunnels. Method of check-
ing lines and levels through 6 inch pipe between North Manhattan
& South Weehawken Tunnels, previous to meeting of North Shields.
Alignment Corps at work in North Manhattan Tunnel.

Jan. 17, 07.

opposite

1.7. The Bergen Hill Tunnels during construction, August 28, 1906. Photograph by the O'Rourke Engineering Construction Company.

1.8. Sandhogs in front of the shield during construction of the Hudson River Tunnels, November 1, 1905.

1.9. Surveyors inside a tube of the Hudson River Tunnels, January 17, 1907.

L 185. P. R. R. Tunnels, N. R. Div. Sect. Gy East. 15ft. 4in. Span Twin Tunnel, cut and cover work looking East from Sta. 194+20.   Jan. 11, 07.

1.10. Manhattan tunnels west of the station site, January 11, 1907. Photograph by the O'Rourke Engineering Construction Company.

L 209. P. R. R. Tunnels, N. R. Div. Sect. Gy East. 15 ft. 4 in. Span Twin Tunnels, looking West from Sta. 193+30, showing timbering and arch centers. Nov. 15, 07.

1.11. Manhattan tunnels showing timbering and arch centers west of the station, November 15, 1907.

Photograph by the O'Rourke Engineering Construction Company.

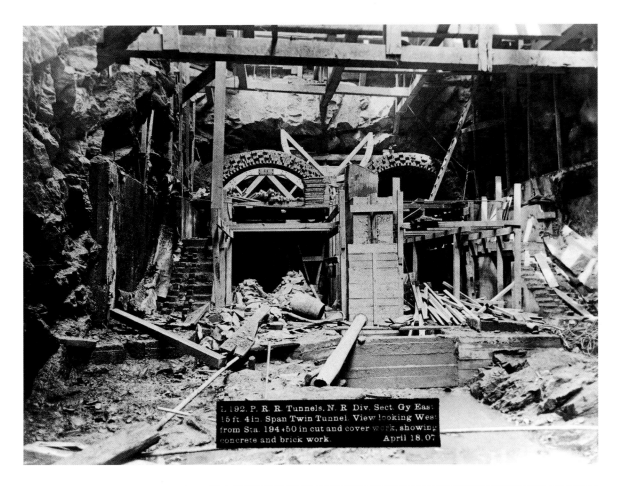

L 192. P. R. R. Tunnels. N. R. Div. Sect. Gy East.
15 ft. 4 in. Span Twin Tunnel. View looking West
from Sta. 194+50 in cut and cover work, showing
concrete and brick work.   April 18, 07.

L 246. P. R. R. Tunnels. N. R. Div. Sect. Gy East. View of East end
of the Gy East Tunnels, above bench level; at junction with Terminal
Station West.   Oct. 23, 08.

put it, "The Pennsylvania extension into New York ranks among the great engineering feats of all time. It is the greatest ever done to get a suitable location for a passenger terminal."[21] Rea insisted on this point. When the railroad's publicist drafted an article entitled "Making New York a Way Station," Rea recalled it. "We are going to expend considerably over $100,000,000 to prevent this very thing. . . . New York City is at present isolated, and all of our plans for the tunnel extension of the New York Connecting Railroad are to make New York a center of commerce and not a way station. All of these steps have been taken because of the fact that New York is the commercial metropolis of the Country." [22]

THE SITE

The paper proposals of the Pennsylvania Railroad showed station sites scattered across lower Manhattan.[23] None of the proposals anticipated the final station site: eight acres bounded by Seventh and Eighth Avenues, 31st and 33rd Streets. Including the trackyard, which extended to Tenth Avenue, the entire site amounted to twenty-eight acres. Engineering breakthroughs made it possible to send trains across the Hudson, but their destination was determined by the familiar law of real estate: the value of a central location.

Though latter-day critics disparaged the site as somewhat marginal, at least compared to Grand Central Station, it seemed close to ideal at the time. It was adjacent to the bustling area around Herald and Greeley Squares which, following the arrival of R. H. Macy & Company in 1901, was taking shape as the new shopping district of Manhattan. The intersection of Broadway and Sixth Avenue was also in the process of becoming a transit node; it was served by the Sixth Avenue Elevated Line and Broadway street cars, and the Hudson and Manhattan Railroad Company (the PATH trains today) was constructing an underground train line to 33rd Street.[24] Thirty-fourth Street, a major crosstown thoroughfare, was traversed by streetcars as was Eighth Avenue, and an elevated line ran along Ninth Avenue. In sum, the site was surrounded by surface and elevated rail lines; more importantly, clean, underground, rapid transit service was in the offing, with construction of the first line of a subway system having begun in 1900. Lines were under consideration for Seventh and Eighth Avenues, a development that the Pennsylvania Railroad strongly advocated. August Belmont, head of the IRT, which built and operated the first line, wanted to build a Seventh Avenue extension from Times Square to Penn Station and downtown. The East Side was dominated by Grand Central whereas the West Side had no passenger train facilities. Any locational disadvantages of Penn Station were not evident at the outset; they evolved over time as a result of the dynam-

1.12. Manhattan tunnels showing concrete and brick work west of the station, April 18, 1907. Photograph by the O'Rourke Engineering Construction Company.

1.13. The portals of the Manhattan tunnels west of the station, October 23, 1908. Photograph by the O'Rourke Engineering Construction Company.

1.14. Pedestrians on 31st Street, c.1903. A crane, barely visible on the left, indicates that clearance of the station site is underway.

ics of urban development, and in particular the delayed construction of subway lines on Seventh and Eighth Avenues which left the West Side underserved by rapid transit.

The station site presented, at worst, two manageable shortcomings. The first were geographical constraints that determined the low level of the tracks. Trains had a relatively short distance in which to climb from a depth of 93 feet, at the low point of the Hudson River tunnel, to Eleventh Avenue where the tracks had to level off. The net effect, once engineers determined the maximum grade tolerable for heavy traffic and fast-moving, multicar trains, was that the tracks at Penn Station had to be depressed unusually far below street level—45 feet, about twice as deep as the subway.[25] This condition—the considerable depth of the railroad tracks—presented the architects of the station with a defining aspect of their design problem: to devise a circulation system that made vertical movement the equivalent of four stories in height both effortless and efficient.

The other negative feature of the site derived from its midtown location: the property was already developed for residential and commercial use. Obviously, undeveloped

land would have been cheaper for the railroad to acquire, but a central location, which
was a pre-condition of the New York extension, inevitably meant high land costs. Moreover, large-scale condemnation in Manhattan raised social issues; the railroad had to
demolish hundreds of tenements and dis-
place thousands of people. Luckily for the
company, it found a neighborhood that was
already condemned in the public's eyes.
"Famous home of vice and blackmail" was
how the *New York Herald* described the Tenderloin in 1903. "Foul Tenderloin! Least
wholesome spot in town, / Where vice and
greed full many a man brought down."[26] Its
nightclubs, bars, and brothels brought the
wrath of reformers, notably the Reverend
Charles Parkhurst of the Madison Square
Presbyterian Church and president of the
Society for the Prevention of Crime, who
stirred public indignation.[27] The Committee
of Fifteen, a citizens' group, that met be-

1.15. Buildings slated for demolition on 32nd Street west of Ninth Avenue, c.1903. Photograph by the O'Rourke Engineering Construction Company.

tween 1900 and 1902 to investigate vice in New York, targeted the Tenderloin. (The committee was chaired by William Baldwin, who had a special interest in the site since he was
president of the Long Island Railroad, a subsidiary of the Pennsylvania Railroad.) The
area was also home to New York's rapidly growing black population (Fig. 1.14). One local
realtor summed up the situation for Rea: "Seventh Avenue has been for many years considered to be like a chinese wall on the west side of the city south of 42nd St.[,] . . . on and
beyond which no respectable man or woman could safely go. It is known as filled with
thugs, bums, and wicked negroes. . . ."[28] Marked by vice, by race, and by class, the
Tenderloin was deemed expendable.

Penn Station was the first urban renewal project in twentieth-century Manhattan. Fritz
Steele's poem conveyed the hope of social reform. "Sunk are your hovels, but in wholesome ruin / Freed from the stigma of much 'shady doing.' / The iron horse has sent your
dives to join / The other nightmares of the Tenderloin."[29] The social dimension of the
renewal project, more specifically the removal of unwanted groups from midtown, helps

1.16. Buildings slated for demolition on 32nd Street, looking west toward the Ninth Avenue Elevated Railroad, c.1903–4. Photograph by the O'Rourke Engineering Construction Company.

to explain the railroad's decision to make no provision for processing immigrants at Penn Station; immigrants were kept out of the station and handled exclusively in Jersey City.[30] Social reformers, business people, and city planners envisioned an affluent neighborhood replacing low-rent shops after the station opened. One newspaper spelled out the vision: "Smart shops and resplendent bazaars will line the new streets and plazas of the old Tenderloin site. Here the wealth and fashion of the metropolis will mingle with crowds from the country, thronging the grand corridors of the palace station, to be whisked between town and country under the floods of Hell Gate and the Hudson with magic speed and luxury. What a change from yesterday, when police protected dives reeked with vice of every kind known from Thirtieth street to ancient Babylon."[31] Ultimately it was advantageous that the station was removed from the current business centers downtown. "To establish a new center which shall serve to divert traffic from the old ones and relieve their congestion, which shall create or enhance values in a neglected and derelict neighborhood is a civic benefaction. . . ." *Architectural Record* summed up prevailing opinion.[32]

The challenge for a giant corporation was to buy a Manhattan neighborhood undercover and without inflating values. The railroad hired a realty company in summer 1901 to appraise the Tenderloin properties and, guided by that schedule of valuations, began to assemble the site before making its plans public in December 1901.[33] The purchasing agents tracked down tenement owners day and night across the city since speed was of the essence. "The buildings in the Terminal zone were occupied by many negroes, saloons, dance halls, gambling joints, and for many other purposes which made the work of those who did the buying not only difficult, but also often dangerous," explained Douglas Robinson, president of the railroad's real estate company. The agents offered the working-class owners irresistible buyouts in cash—a payment of $5,000 on the spot with the balance paid in cash on delivery of the deed within thirty days. The railroad managed to conceal its involvement from its purchasing agents as well as from the Tenderloin property owners for about sixty days, during which time the bulk of the property was acquired. According to Robinson, over one hundred lots were purchased in only two weeks. "It is doubtful whether so large a tract, involving so many owners, was ever before bought in a city."[34]

1.17. Buildings slated for demolition on Ninth Avenue at the corner of 32nd Street, c.1903. The sign in the corner shop reads "Removal Sale." Photograph by the O'Rourke Engineering Construction Company.

About five hundred buildings were demolished in 1903, and five to six thousand people were forced to move (Figs. 1.15–17).[35] The house wreckers paid the Pennsylvania Railroad a fee entitling them to salvage building material, including sidewalk flagging, from the buildings they demolished.[36] The Pennsylvania Railroad did not pay relocation expenses, with one exception. After demolishing the Church of St. Michael, which stood on Ninth Avenue between 31st and 32nd Streets, the railroad rebuilt the church on a nearby site.[37] The last building standing was a pub, no doubt serving demolition crews until the end; it is visible in an extraordinary photograph by H. B. Gates of the momentarily vacant site in 1904 (Fig. 1.18). The photograph also documents West 32nd Street, arguably the railroad's most significant purchase. In May 1902, the Pennsylvania Railroad proposed

1.18. View of the station site along 32nd Street, looking east from the Ninth Avenue Elevated Railroad, 1904. House wreckers have removed all but one building, a bar on Eighth Avenue. Photograph by H. B. Gates.

the following terms to transit officials (the Board of Rapid Transit Commissioners): "We would respectfully suggest that a rental be charged for the two blocks of 32nd St. which we ask to have closed, based upon a valuation arrived at by applying to the area taken the average price per square foot which this Company has paid for abutting property, after deducting the value of the buildings." Although the formula offered a very narrow measure of the value of a public street, the city accepted the deal. In lieu of rent, the railroad made a lump-sum payment of $788,600 for 32nd Street.[38]

Excavation began in July 1904 (Figs. 1.19–20). It went down 75 feet to the bedrock of Manhattan. Eighth and Ninth Avenues, their rail lines, and the underlying infrastructure of the city—pipes, sewers, electrical wires, and other conduits—were supported by massive trestles. The excavated material—3 million cubic yards of mostly solid rock—was taken by train to a temporary wharf on 32nd Street and ferried by barge to Greenville, New

1.19. Excavation of station site looking west from approximately 33rd Street and Seventh Avenue, c.1904–5. Eighth and Ninth Avenues are supported on trestles in the midground, and the site of the power house, on the south side of 31st Street (at left), is already enclosed by the concrete retaining wall. Photograph by Brown Brothers.

1.20. Construction site facing east, July 8, 1907. The view shows, from left to right, the bedrock of Manhattan, Seventh Avenue supported on stilts, the concrete retaining wall, and the first elements of the steel frame.

Jersey, where it was used as fill for a freight yard under construction by the Pennsylvania Railroad.[39] A massive concrete retaining wall was built around the perimeter of the site in conjunction with the intricate rethreading of the city's sewer, water, and gas mains. Five feet thick at the top, the sloped retaining wall reached a thickness of up to 30 feet at the bottom—a concrete fortress to guard the carefully timed movement of trains.

THE ARCHITECTURAL COMMISSION

At a meeting in his Philadelphia office on April 24, 1902, Alexander Cassatt commissioned Charles McKim to design the new station.[40] McKim's excitement about the opportunity to design Manhattan's largest building comes across even in the tersely phrased telegrams he sent his partner, William Rutherford Mead, and his friend, Charles Moore, with whom he was working on a plan for Washington, D.C. But McKim tactfully struck an apologetic note with Daniel H. Burnham, whom Cassatt had commissioned a year earlier to design Union Station in the nation's capital. Penn Station was "unsought, and . . . came as a complete surprise," McKim wrote Burnham. "They should have given it to you, and I fully expected they would. Just after the interview, [I learned] . . . that they employed a New York man as a question of policy, and I ascribe our appointment chiefly to this cause."[41]

McKim was unduly modest. By virtue of the size of his firm and its productivity, McKim, Mead & White was uniquely qualified to handle the extensive demands imposed by a project as large as Pennsylvania Station. Except for Burnham, no other American architect had McKim's depth of experience in designing civic buildings and urban ensembles; none was as involved in the development of New York City. From the Brooklyn Museum and Grand Army Plaza to the clutch of private clubs in midtown Manhattan and north to the Morningside campus of Columbia University, McKim played a crucial role in shaping the monumental landscape of the city. Yet the most useful preparation for Penn Station may have been his work a year earlier on the plan of Washington, D.C.

In 1901 Daniel Burnham enlisted McKim to serve on the Senate Park Commission, which was established by the U.S. Senate to develop an improvement plan for Washington, D.C. The purpose of the commission was to renew the monumental vision of L'Enfant's original plan, which haphazard growth had undermined, and to propose new arrangements of parks and public buildings in the city center. McKim's work on the Senate Park Commission influenced his response to the Pennsylvania Station commission in two respects. First, the search for a monumental vocabulary appropriate for Washington, D.C. reoriented McKim's interests from Renaissance palaces, which had inspired earlier designs such as the University Club in New York City, to ancient and baroque structures whose large scale and stately grandeur he considered fitting for federal buildings. Second, the Washington work involved McKim in planning a new train station. One of the major achievements of the Senate Park Commission was the removal of a railroad station owned by the Pennsylvania Railroad from the middle of the Mall, which was accomplished when Alexander Cassatt agreed to build a new station on its own plaza. Although Burnham designed the new Union Station, McKim was a coequal participant in the preliminary planning process; they shared the same vision of railroad stations as monumental embellishments. The members of the Senate Park Commission went on a study tour of Europe in the summer of 1901 and honed their ideas in response to ancient Roman buildings and nineteenth-century train stations. It was probably during this trip that McKim collected the prints and photographs in his album of European railroad stations to which he eventually added pictures of Penn Station.

A week after obtaining the commission for Pennsylvania Station in April 1902, McKim sent his first sketches to Rea. Neither those early sketches nor any other drawing by McKim survives. The only clues about the starting point of McKim's design process come from two telegrams he sent to Rea. One indicates that the tripartite division of the train concourse was fixed at the outset. "Drawings scale fifty feet to one inch will show covered tracks[,] as requested train shed in three spans moderate height." The other telegram confirms the railroad's initial intention to build a hotel above the station. "North and South axis of station hotel taken on centre of proposed street running through to Thirty-fourth Street, according to your blue print."[42] Positioned in the middle of the site, the hotel was aligned with a walkway piercing through the block north of the station and providing an outlet on 34th Street.

A hotel was more than a convenience for travelers and a boon for traffic; it was an investment to amortize the costs of the station. The Hudson Terminal Buildings, for example, brought in close to a million dollars a year. Pennsylvania Station, on the other hand, was built "absolutely without regard to real estate possibilities," in the words of the *Wall Street Journal*. What accounted for the railroad's apparently uneconomic decision? Art historians generally credit McKim's classical architectural vision and his antimodern dislike of towers. While these were surely contributory factors, it seems unlikely that the Pennsylvania Railroad made a key financial decision on the basis of aesthetic factors alone. "The fact remains," the *Wall Street Journal* pointed out, "that the Pennsylvania people adopted their plan only after thoroughly considering the real estate proposition, and upon the best advice obtainable, and rejected it as unwise in their particular case." Unwise because to maximize operational efficiency and provide for future growth, the Pennsylvania required twenty-one train tracks. "Considerable time was devoted to devising a large building overlying the terminal and tracks, in whole or in part, but to have put it there, even by resorting to gun metal and other extremities for support, would have cut out two or more tracks, equivalent to one-tenth of the terminal, and filled that space with numerous large columns which would have impaired the future efficiency of the station. . . . The Pennsylvania's directors felt that they could not cover the ground with anything more rentable than the present structure without making the railroad business a secondary feature."[43] The absolute priority of the Pennsylvania Railroad was the railroad business. On that basis and with the encouragement of McKim, the railroad abandoned the on-site hotel.

The evolution of McKim's design is something of a mystery since the earliest images of the station—photographs of a plaster model displayed at the Louisiana Purchase Exposition in 1904 (Fig. 1.21) (the model no longer survives) and a suite of thirteen presentation drawings by Jules Crow from 1905 to 1906—already show it in nearly final form. In failing health and dispirited by Stanford White's murder in June 1906, McKim shortly thereafter withdrew from active practice. Responsibility for the station passed to William Symmes Richardson, who had been elevated to the rank of partner in January 1906. Richardson was in charge during construction of the station building, which began in June 1906, and was responsible for the late refinements in the design, including ornamental detail.[44] In addition, Richardson probably drafted, with input from McKim, the firm's explanation of the design, which was cited in the Pennsylvania Railroad's publicity and in the extensive journalistic coverage of the new station. By the time the building was inaugurated on September 10, 1910, sadly both Cassatt and McKim were dead.

CONSTRUCTION

The construction photographs may well be the most revealing documentation of Penn Station (Figs. 1.22–37). Photographers systematically recorded the building process, beginning with the erection of the first portion of the steel frame, at the southeast corner of the station. When McKim, Mead & White hired Louis H. Dreyer, a commercial photographer, in 1908 to take construction photos, they insisted only on the need for serial documentation: "Dear Sir: Will you kindly make three exposures of the Pennsylvania Station work at Seventh Avenue and 31st Street on the eleventh of each month until further notice, from the same points as those taken by you on the eleventh of September."[45] The construction photos were probably made for liability protection, to serve as documentation in the event of disputes with contractors, but even if the purpose was banal, the results were often visually spectacular, at least in the case of Dreyer's work.

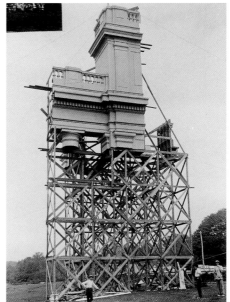

1.22. The steel frame of Pennsylvania Station at the corner of 31st Street and Seventh Avenue, November 25, 1907. The old street lamps were replaced by fixtures designed by McKim, Mead & White.

1.23. The steel frame of the waiting hall, July 7, 1908.

1.24. Full-scale model of the facade of Pennsylvania Station showing the relationship of the crowning features, c.1906. McKim had the model built to study the proportions of his design.

1.25. Seventh Avenue facade during construction, August 13, 1908. Two structural systems were used in the facade: the columns were load bearing whereas the pilasters and masonry walls were built with granite panels attached to the steel frame.

1.26. Seventh Avenue facade from 33rd Street during construction, September 11, 1908.
The bundle of conduits in the foreground traverse the future site of the Hotel Pennsylania. Photograph by Louis Dreyer.

1.27. View from Eighth Avenue,
September 11, 1908.
Photograph by Louis Dreyer.

His series of seventy-eight large-format photographs stands apart from the other construction pictures of the station by unknown photographers. The latter pictures are smaller, sometimes blurry, haphazardly composed, and of strictly documentary interest. Dreyer's photographs have crisp detail, striking compositions, and rich sepia tones that give them a compelling visual quality. In his shots from the roof of Penn Station, you can see clear to the Hudson River, while close-up views reveal the stratigraphy of conduits below the street. The clarity of vision is crystalline, and the condition of the photographs pristine. Dreyer consistently photographed the Seventh and Eighth Avenue facades from fixed points of view, as his client requested, but his pictures of the concourse are more numerous and were taken from a wider variety of positions. They evoke the photographer's fascination with the vaulting structure of this great space as well as the variety of construction methods on view. The pictures show the wooden frames used for centering masonry arches juxtaposed with the skeletal steel frame. Large wooden scaffolds for the

1.28. View from the scaffold of the waiting hall looking east, across the north baggage courtyard, March 22, 1909. Photograph by Louis Dreyer.

1.29. The train concourse looking southwest, April 17, 1909. Photograph by Louis Dreyer.

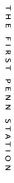

N.Y. TERMINAL
OF
P.T & T.R.R.
APRIL 19 TH 1909.
FROM MAIN SCAFFOLD
LOOKING WEST.
L.H. DREYER. PHOTO.

1.30. The roof of the train concourse from the scaffold of the waiting hall looking west, April 19, 1909. The large rectangular pit in the distance is the future site of the General Post Office. Photograph by Louis Dreyer.

1.31. Rooftop view of the train concourse and waiting hall, June 14, 1909. Photograph by Louis Dreyer.

1.32. The train concourse looking northeast, July 12, 1909. Photograph by Louis Dreyer.

1.33. View from a train platform showing the covered third rail and staircases leading to the train concourse, December 9, 1909.

1.34. Atop the scaffold where plaster coffers were cast and attached to the steel truss, December 28, 1909.

1.35. Scaffold used for casting and hanging the plaster coffers of the waiting hall, February 10, 1910.

use of riveters encase the structural columns, and segments of arched trusses hang like branches in the air. The surprising pairings of traditional and modern building techniques in Dreyer's concourse pictures seem to capture the very essence of McKim's design.

The construction photographs underscore a point that was easy to forget once the building was completed: that Penn Station was a steel skeleton with curtain-wall construction. A grid of 650 concrete-covered steel piers, spaced around the train tracks, carried the weight of the structure down to bedrock. Above these footings rose a complex steel structure that took the engineers about two years to design. Granite was cut in panels and fastened to the metal structure; unlike Low Library at Columbia University and other earlier buildings by McKim, Mead & White, the walls of Penn Station were not load bearing. The architects worried mostly about two aspects of construction: obtaining an adequate supply of granite, and fitting it to the struc-

ture. They explained the problem to George Gibbs: "We were confronted with the condition of quarrying and cutting granite for a building of intricate steel design without any of the necessary steel plans to show the amount of the back cutting, etc. necessary to fit the granite to the steel."[46] The amount of granite needed for the station—a half-million cubic feet—pushed the quarries in Milford, Massachusetts, to their limit and forced a reorganization of the local industry. But ultimately the pace of masonry work satisfied the architects: the stone was set in thirteen months, an average of 10,000 cubic feet per week.[47] All indications are that the George A. Fuller Construction Company, under the direction of Paul Starrett, did a masterly job executing this complex task.

The one exception to the modern construction was the exterior columns, which were solid granite. The eight giant columns of the waiting hall were hollow, consisting of thin shells of fluted stone wrapped around and pinned to an interior steel support. No con-

1.36. View at track level from Column #100 looking northwest, January 19, 1910. A grid of 650 concrete-covered steel columns supported the station above the tracks. Photograph by Louis Dreyer.

1.37. Stonecarvers with keystones for Pennsylvania Station, c. 1907. The keystones were used in the thermal windows of the waiting hall.

struction photographs recorded this condition (whether none were taken or none survive is not known), so the truth about these columns was not revealed until the station was demolished (see fig. 2.11). The structural reality was that the steel members inside the columns supported the ceiling truss and that the arched surfaces of the ceiling that looked like vaults were not built as such. McKim achieved a correspondence between the actual steel structure and the represented masonry structure in other ways: the inner mullions of the large thermal windows were aligned with steel supports, and the stone pilasters were coordinated with the bays of the steel frame. But the waiting hall created a tectonic illusion: that the columns supported the weight of the lofty vault and that forces were channeled through a traditional masonry system. The deep, octagonal ceiling coffers were cast in plaster from molds on a scaffold and hung from the frame with steel anchors. The plaster was colored slightly so that the tone of the ceiling would blend with the travertine walls. One more illusion: most of the travertine was not real travertine. Although promotional literature boasted that Penn Station was the first building in America to use travertine from the very quarries used in ancient Rome, the actual stone was used sparingly, reserved for pilaster bases and low-lying trim. McKim, Mead & White drew up a recipe for synthetic stone that was mixed on site; it was obviously cheaper and easier to supply than travertine.[48]

Some critics, both in McKim's lifetime and later, complained about his structural inauthenticity. At Low Library, the centerpiece of Columbia University, McKim proposed a concrete dome supported by iron trusses. William Ware, dean of the school of architecture, objected to the truss supports since they did not conform to traditional methods of dome construction. Low Library was "not a real dome . . . only an ingenious contrivance to produce the effect of one."[49] Ware was right. McKim was willing to abandon the building methods of the ancients. In Penn Station, he embraced modern building techniques and successfully exploited them precisely to achieve ancient tectonic and spatial effects.

THE DESIGN

Pennsylvania Station did not aim to please (Fig. 1.38). It aimed to impress, to overwhelm, and to dignify the visitor through the grandeur of its architectural forms and the ceremonial quality of its plan. Penn Station did not make you feel comfortable; it made you feel important.

The last major building McKim designed, Penn Station was also his crowning achievement. The station epitomizes his approach to design problems, which was to tap the past for relevant historical models. Three building types informed the design of Penn Station: the columnar entry gate, the ancient bath, and the glass-and-iron train shed. McKim manipulated and combined those prototypes to produce a design that captured their spirit without strictly copying their forms. This method did not yield aesthetically adventurous buildings, but that was not McKim's goal. "Confidence," he explained, "comes not from inspiration but from knowledge."[50] His method yielded buildings like Penn Station that were intelligent, elegant, and venerable even when brand new.

History guided McKim's design process, yet Penn Station made him confront the modern world. It was not just that Penn Station owed its existence to modern technologies—to electricity, which made it possible to run trains underground, and to steel-

1.38. Pennsylvania Station from the rooftop of R. H. Macy & Co., March 4, 1910. Photograph by Louis Dreyer.

frame construction, which allowed McKim's to build monumental forms above train tracks. The social program of the station was inextricably linked with modern urban life. The station was meant to accommodate enormous crowds, facilitate efficient movement, and reinforce daily schedules that measured every minute of the day. The numerous clocks regulating life within Penn Station were symptomatic of a preoccupation with time and efficiency in the city at large. Neither the Boston Public Library nor Columbia University, McKim's two other outstanding achievements in the realm of civic architecture, engaged modern technologies, modern modes of thought, and modern urban forces to the same extent as Pennsylvania Station.

Because the station traded in the currency of modern life—speed, time, and efficiency—it presented a challenge to McKim's backward-looking orientation and his views of the social order. McKim's sympathies lay with the elite class for whom he created private clubs and town houses, spaces conducive to refined sociability. He did not picture the general public hurrying for trains, but "well-gowned women, who would sweep up and down his broad staircases," a like-minded friend observed.[51] McKim disliked the commercial culture of the metropolis, its crowded streets, and high-rise towers. New York City was dedicated to the vertical dimension; he preferred the horizontal. McKim described his disenchantment with Manhattan in a letter to Lawrence Grant White, Stanford White's son, written on May 18, 1909, as Penn Station approached completion.

The New Metropolitan Life Insurance tower, 700 feet high, makes the Flatiron Building look like a toy and puts every building within a mile in the shade. But all the same, Madison Square Tower [designed by Stanford White], one third of its height, is as far the greater of the two as David than Goliath. The first has the merit of bigness, and that's all. I think the skyline of New York grows daily more hideous. A recent law provides for the widening of Fifth Avenue by narrowing the sidewalks. This involves the removal of areas, front stoops, and all projections into the sidewalk; and you can imagine how beautiful is the result. . . . The constantly increasing traffic on the streets and crowded sidewalks has made this imperative, and I suppose it is a choice of evils that must be accepted. What New York is coming to, Dieu sait [God knows]! And He won't tell. But you can imagine.[52]

McKim responded to hideous New York in his design of Pennsylvania Station. His talents were perfected in this building, but also stretched to the limit owing to its fundamental challenge. The architect's antimodern outlook had to cope with the quintessential modernity of the metropolitan train station.

Stirred by an uneasiness in hideous New York, McKim was not content to meet the railroad's functional demands. While amply equipping Penn Station to sort and handle vast numbers of people and trains, and to sustain the fast-paced life of the city, McKim tried to temper the brute claims of efficiency with the reassuring comforts of historical tradition. Guided by a vision of civic grandeur, he translated the mundane business of boarding trains into a stately procession, and subsumed the commotion of constant movement and disorganized crowds into the station's overriding order. "One does not rush to catch a Pennsylvania train—one proceeds to it in orderly but expeditious manner," a critic observed.[53] McKim achieved this sense of orderly flow by creating an orchestrated sequence of three distinctive spaces that compelled the traveler to move forward and down to tracks forty-five feet below street level without suffering any strain from that considerable descent. These powerful architectural forms transmuted an activity that was normally hectic, disorderly, and crowded into a controlled, ceremonial procession, and they imparted a sense of dignity to all travelers, not only the aristocratic types whom he principally had in mind.

Yet for all its artful references to the past, the station was not a stultifying essay in refined historicism. Historical elements were interwoven with steel truss, plate glass, and the power of electricity and of locomotion. These elements collaborated in an architectural drama with a surprising climax: what looked, from the outside, like an age-old monument of stone was, at its heart, a throbbing hub of movement in glass and steel. But this drama did not imply a conflict between past and present. Rather it demonstrated their seamless connection and the enduring relevance of the classical language of architecture. McKim converted his ambivalence about the new age that was dawning into an affirmation of the value of history, and forged stone and steel, ceremony and efficiency, order and motion into a creative alliance. Pennsylvania Station was a heroic building and a great work of art because it brought these opposing values together.

The public statements of McKim, Mead & White did not acknowledge this ambivalence. They offered a different, more reassuring explanation for the size and imperial character of the station. "The conditions of modern American life, in which undertakings of great magnitude and scale are carried through, involving interests in all parts of the world, are more nearly akin to the life of the Roman Empire than that of any other known civilization. It seemed, therefore, fitting and appropriate in every way that the type of architecture adopted should be a development from Roman models, and while the building is of necessity, on account of the requirements of its uses, different from any building known to have been previously built, its inspiration can be directly traced to the great buildings of the Roman Empire."[54] This statement did not explain McKim's artistic intentions. Nonetheless, it was true. Pennsylvania Station embodied the imperial grandeur and self-confidence of America at the turn of the century.

The exterior of Penn Station was forbidding. *Architectural Record* found it monotonous and gloomy, suggestive of a house of detention. Part of the problem was the large size of the building. Each facade stretched a full two city blocks—430 feet on the avenues, 734 feet on the side streets. At least New York's other jumbo buildings occupying several city blocks—the American Museum of Natural History, the Metropolitan Museum of Art, the New York Public Library—were located in parks and set back from the sidewalk so that pedestrians were shielded from the full impact of their bulk. However, the size of Penn Station was less significant than McKim's chosen vocabulary of Imperial Roman classicism. The facades of Pennsylvania Station were an essay in monumental expression, a language familiar enough in ancient Rome or Washington, D.C. but strange in New York City, where streetscapes were typically animated by varied, smaller units with a well-defined ground floor. Skyscrapers rising elsewhere in Manhattan were certainly taller, but Penn Station embodied the idea of bigness and mass—on a horizontal plane.

1.39. Union Station, Washington, D.C., by Daniel Burnham, 1903–8. Photograph by Brown Brothers.

From the outside, it looked like no other train station. Some stations, like the old Grand Central, pretended to be palaces with multistory facades. Others had long, arcaded fronts. The arcade was the most popular type of facade because it offered travelers the convenience of multiple entrances while adumbrating the vaulted form of the train sheds inside. Daniel Burnham pursued this approach at Union Station in Washington, D.C., where an arcade flanks a triumphal arch, inspired by the ancient Roman sites he had visited with McKim (Fig. 1.39). Although sympathetic to Burnham's goals, McKim chose a radically different image for his New York station.

Instead of arches, Pennsylvania Station had a row of austere granite columns along the Seventh Avenue facade (Fig. 1.40). The columns were massive: thirty-five feet high, four and a half feet in diameter, each drum weighing four to six tons and unfluted in order to reinforce their bulk. McKim selected the Doric order because of its strength and simplicity, but he revised the order to make it even more severe. In addition to the plain treatment of the columns, all surfaces were smooth and unadorned, including the pediments and the entablature, although the Doric order normally called for a triglyph frieze. McKim eliminated distracting surface decoration so as to focus attention on the build-

1.40. Seventh Avenue facade of Pennsylvania Station, February 18, 1910. Photograph by Louis Dreyer.

1.41. Grand Central Terminal, c. 1915. Photograph by Brown Brothers.

ing's monumental scale and mass, an effect reinforced by the lighting effects that draped the colonnade in darkness from the rear. The exterior of Pennsylvania Station had no frill or flash, no crowd-pleasing decorative splendor as at Grand Central Terminal with its garlands, cornucopia, and exuberant figures (Fig. 1.41). The decorative features on the main facade of Penn Station were limited to the crowning balustrade, the eagles standing at attention, and the subdued figures of Day and Night beside the central clock (Fig. 1.42). What enlivens the facade is not decoration but the projections of the colonnade, which demarcate entrances to the station: the center portico was for pedestrians, the pedimented porticos at the ends for vehicles. The columns of the three porticos are arranged in a double file, which intensifies the monumental and daunting impression of the building at the points of entry. Unlike Mc-Kim's earlier buildings, notably the Boston Public Library, which have intricate and pleasing surface effects, this late work elim-

1.42. Statues of Day and Night by Adolf Weinman and the clock above the main entrance to Pennsylvania Station, 1964. The four entrances on the cross axes of the station were crowned by identical statues. Day holds a garland of sunflowers and looks out alertly, while the semi-naked figure of Night wears a cloak on her head and looks down to signify the onset of darkness. Three eagles stood at attention on each side of the central trio. Photograph by Norman McGrath.

1.43. The Propylaea of the Acropolis, Athens. Photograph by William Stillman, 1882, from an album of Charles McKim.

1.44. The Colonnade of St. Peter's, Rome, by Gianlorenzo Bernini, 1656–67.

inated surface and texture. It is all about mass and volume, solid and void. The effect is powerful but uninviting.

McKim harnessed these formal effects to give Pennsylvania Station "the appearance of a monumental gateway and entrance to one of the great Metropolitan cities of the world."[55] "Monumental gateway" was not a figure of speech; it meant a specific architectural idea defined by the Propylaea, the columnar entrance to the Acropolis in Athens. McKim knew the site well, from both his travels and the extraordinary photographs of William Stillman, which he collected. Figure 1.43 belongs to a series of rare prints from Stillman's photographic campaign of the Acropolis in about 1882 that McKim kept in an album of architectural source material.

The six-column centerpiece of Penn Station descends from the Propylaea and its offspring, in particular the Brandenburg Gate (1789–94) in Berlin. But in order to transform the idea of a monumental gateway into an elongated facade, McKim looked to two other models, pictures of which were pinned above his drafting table: Bernini's Colonnade

in the piazza in front of St. Peter's in Rome (Fig. 1.44) and John Soane's Bank of England in London. According to Charles Moore, McKim became entranced by Bernini's Colonnade when the members of the Senate Park Commission visited Rome in June 1901, and it is easy to see echoes of Bernini at Penn Station—in the Doric order and undecorated frieze, the crowning balustrade, the projecting porticos, and the use of pediments as framing elements of the facade.

McKim looked to Soane's Bank of England for guidance in differentiating the street facades of the station. One element is repeated: in the middle of each facade a projecting portico, identical to the one on Seventh Avenue, articulates an entrance. Otherwise, the facades follow a clear hierarchy, measured by the allocation of columns. The hierarchy progresses from the open, sculptural treatment of the Seventh Avenue facade to the

1.45. View along 31st Street, 1910. Photograph by De W. C. Ward.

1.46. Eighth Avenue facade of Pennsylvania Station, March 4, 1910. The site of the Post Office appears in the lower right corner. Photograph by Louis Dreyer.

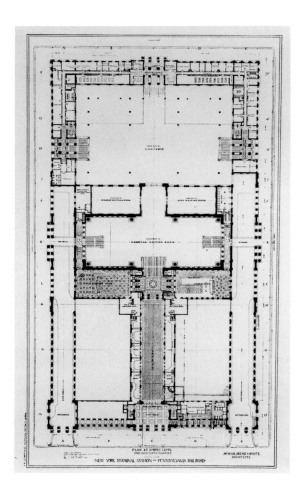

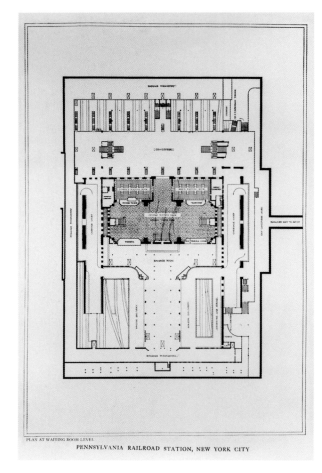

facades facing 31st and 33rd Streets, where pilastered walls frame a row of columns that illuminate the internal driveways (see Figs. 1.38 and 1.45). Except for the center portico, the Eighth Avenue facade is entirely enclosed and flat, and reads decidedly as the back entrance (Fig. 1.46). The architectural hierarchy was at odds with the functional program of the station, which stressed accessibility in all directions. A traveler could, indeed, enter from any side, but the architecture privileged the Seventh Avenue entrance, both on the outside and within.

THE INTERIOR PROCESSION

The severe grandeur of the facade implied a code of conduct; it called for decorous and dignified behavior, and that expectation was reinforced by the formal plan (Figs. 1.47 and 1.48). A visitor encountered a series of three major spaces. A commercial arcade extended the axis of 32nd Street to the middle of the station. It led to the general waiting hall,

PENNSYLVANIA STATION
of
P. T. & T. R. R.
SEPT. 11TH 1909
MAIN ARCADE   LOOKING EAST
L.H.DREYER PHOTO.

which was oriented perpendicular to the arcade and extended nearly the full width of the station. The procession culminated in the train concourse, an adaptation of the traditional train shed, which provided access to the tracks. These three spaces were enclosed by a rectangular ring of buildings that fronted on the city streets; although the peripheral buildings established the public face of the station, they primarily housed offices and were restricted to railroad personnel. The overall arrangement of three main spaces inside an enclosing wall reflects the layout of ancient Roman baths, a model that also influenced the design of the waiting hall.

The plan of Penn Station was logical, symmetric, and straightforward, yet the experience of walking through the building was full of surprises. McKim dramatized the procession from one space to the next through contrasting architectural effects: solid and transparent, sculptural and flat, dim and bright. Indeed, the architectural richness of the procession from the Seventh Avenue entrance to the tracks was unsurpassed in McKim's work and captures something of the drama of baroque architecture he observed in Rome.

1.49. Commercial arcade facing the main entrance on Seventh Avenue, September 11, 1909. Note the wall of glass at the entrance. Photograph by Louis Dreyer.

1.50. The shop front of Huyler's Candies in the commercial arcade, c.1910.

1.51. Lunch counter, 1910. Photograph by De W. C. Ward.

After passing between the massive granite columns on Seventh Avenue and into a dim vestibule, pedestrians encountered a transparent and weightless wall made of plate glass. The sharp contrast of stone and glass at the point of entry announced two different structural systems that McKim sought to integrate: the load-bearing masonry system of the colonnade and the steel-frame construction associated with the glass curtain wall. Beyond the glass entry wall was the arcade, offsetting the weightiness of the main facade (Fig. 1.49). The arcade was lofty and brilliantly illuminated by large semi-circular windows cut into the vault. Light reflected in the glass storefronts and on the smooth, cream-colored walls of travertine and plaster (Fig. 1.50). The arcade pointed one's sights to a series of spaces partially revealed through a pair of freestanding columns and the arch above—a vista that drew you on.

The columns marked the entrance to a vestibule, with entrances to the station's two main restaurants: the dining room to the south and the lunchroom to the north (Fig. 1.51; also see Fig. 2.8). The restaurants had flat coffered ceilings and fluted pilasters, giving the rectangular halls a texture and materiality distinct from the arcade. The restaurants as well as the shops in the arcade were lit by windows overlooking interior courtyards covered by skylights that brought natural light to the train tracks below (see Fig. 1.28). The vestibule was a transitional space; it was dimly lit and nearly square to counter the directional force of the rooms on either side. It provided a moment to pause and prepare for the grand descent into the waiting hall.

The waiting hall was a billowing, overwhelming space (Figs. 1.52 and 1.53). "The largest room of its kind in existence," boasted the promotional literature: 300 feet long, 110 feet wide, with groin vaults rising to 150 feet. Eight semi-circular windows, each 72 feet in diameter, flooded the room with light, and eight gigantic Corinthian columns, 60 feet

1.52. Waiting hall facing the 33rd Street entrance, 1910. The staircase at right leads to the commercial arcade.

1.53. Waiting hall facing the 31st Street entrance with information desk at right and ticket counters at left, 1910. The doors at floor level lead to the driveway. The stairs lead to 31st Street.

1.54. Men's waiting room, 1910. Photograph by De W. C. Ward.

1.55. Long Island Railroad waiting room, 1910. This room was on the level of the exit concourse. Photograph by De W. C. Ward.

tall, appeared to support the three bays of the vault. The ticket windows and telephone booths were the only elements at a human scale. The room was large enough to contain City Hall, a point *Scientific American* illustrated on a magazine cover, and larger than the nave of St. Peter's. "Doubtless we are dealing with a 'big thing,'" *Architectural Record* unsympathetically put it.[56]

The waiting hall was twenty feet below street level, a vertical drop reflected in the height of the column pedestals. Travelers arriving by car were able to enter the waiting hall at floor level because the driveways were ramped down; however, pedestrians had to descend a broad flight of stairs. The vault came into view as they were descending, a countermotion that magnified the sense of vertical expansion in the waiting hall. For those approaching from the arcade, the directional contrast in the waiting hall also created a sense of space exploding horizontally. The freestanding, fluted Corinthian columns and robust curls of the acanthus leaves, the strongly projecting entablature blocks and layered ceiling coffers — these sculptural features made the weightless volume of the waiting hall seem weighty. Like the plenitude of a sheltering night sky, the enormous space was both humbling and uplifting.

Big as the waiting hall was, it had no room for seats, which meant it was unsuitable for waiting. To sit, there were three smaller waiting rooms: one for men and one for women on the west side of the waiting hall, and one for the LIRR at a lower level (Figs. 1.54 and 1.55). In October 1910, shortly after the building opened, the superintendent of the station recommended placing 350 seats in the waiting hall. "These seats will more or less obstruct the passage through this room but should cause no great inconvenience to our patrons," Gibbs agreed, noting that there were fewer seats at Penn Station than at the Jersey City terminal where people customarily sat on the floor. I do not wish "to be the advocate of anything that detracts from the appearance of the station, but when our patrons demand a place to sit (as unquestionably they will) we ought to be ready." Rea authorized the installation of extra seats in the LIRR waiting room, but not in the waiting hall.[57] His response shows the commitment of the station's founding fathers to McKim's vision of the misnamed waiting hall, which was not a lounge but more like a crossroads for assembly and movement, a miniature urban hub.

Why was the waiting hall so big? McKim had two basic reasons: the hall referred to two big building types, the ancient Roman bath and the nineteenth-century train shed. The waiting hall of Pennsylvania Station was McKim's response to an ancient ruin that had enthralled him on a trip to Rome in June 1901: the *frigidarium* or cold-water bathing hall of the Baths of Caracalla. Although the visit of the Senate Park Commission preceded the Penn Station commission, McKim saw a connection between the baths and the modern train station, as Moore makes clear.

One particularly hot afternoon, as the quartette [McKim, Burnham, Moore, and Frederick Law Olmsted, Jr.] reclined in the shade of the towering brick walls and arches that remain of the once luxurious Baths of Caracalla, the talk fell on an approaching meeting with President Cassatt that had been arranged in London, and the probabilities that he would yield to persuasion and move the Pennsylvania Station back to a location south of the Mall. . . . Burnham could not imagine that within four years, he would be building a station finer in itself and finer in its location than any other ever built [Union Station in Washington, D.C.]. Nor could McKim dream that he would be called upon to design as a gateway to the American metropolis, the largest building ever constructed at one time, with one of its rooms as big as the nave of Saint Peter's. . . . Looking back to that afternoon, it seems as if the very spirit of Rome—its ordered bigness, its grandeur, its essence of the eternal—stole into their souls. . . .[58]

1.56. Reconstruction of the *frigidarium* of the Baths of Caracalla by G. Abel Blouet, 1828.

The Baths of Caracalla (206–217) were the best preserved of the ancient baths in Rome; still they were in ruinous condition. McKim responded to their scale and imagined them filled with people. Moore reported that he hired "willing but astonished workmen to pose among the ruins to give scale and movement" as he made sketches (they do not survive).[59] He may well have measured the space, but only towering walls remained. The columns and vault were gone. McKim's ideas about the specific features of the bathing hall were informed by nineteenth-century reconstructions, a specialty of the Ecole des Beaux-Arts, where McKim got his professional training (Fig. 1.56).[60] Yet neither in Penn Station nor in any other design did McKim faithfully reconstruct an historic building. In this case,

1.57. Exterior view of the train station in Cologne, Germany, from an album of Charles McKim.

opposite
1.58. View of Pennsylvania Station from Sixth Avenue along 32nd Street, rendering, c.1910.

1.59. Train concourse facing northwest, 1910. Photograph by De W. C. Ward.

he borrowed selected forms—the columnar screens at the short ends of the hall, the freestanding colossal columns along the long walls, the lunette windows, and the groin vault. He evoked the scale of the ruins, making the waiting hall even larger than the classical prototype, and freely designed the décor.[61]

McKim chose the ancient bath as model because he recognized a parallel social function with the modern railroad station. "For inspiration," McKim, Mead & White explained, "the great buildings of ancient Rome were studied, and in particular such buildings as the baths of Caracalla, of Titus, and of Diocletian, and the Basilica of Constantine, which are the greatest examples in architectural history of large, roofed-in areas adapted to assemblages of people."[62] McKim envisioned the waiting hall as the modern equivalent, the place where the largest number of people in the city was likely to gather. The railroad lines populated the station and made it a bustling urban center. How fitting that Jules Guerin decorated the upper walls of the waiting hall with painted maps of the Pennsylvania and Long Island Railroad systems as well as the United States and the world.

The size of the waiting hall, and in particular its height, was also intended to make a visual connection between Penn Station and the familiar form of arched train sheds (Fig. 1.57). McKim's first design goal was to create a monumental gateway; his second goal was to express the building's railroad function. The second aim was conservative inasmuch as McKim wanted to preserve recognizable features of the traditional train station despite fundamental changes in its operation. The age of clean, smoke-free, electric trains eliminated the need for tall open-ended sheds that served to ventilate steam locomotives. The underground tracks of Penn Station did not mandate any form of external expression, but McKim had no interest in inventing a new form to fit revised functional requirements. His aim was to preserve the architectural legibility of the traditional train station: "The exposed train shed, with its large, semicircular ends of glass, has become during the last century a form recognized by the layman as a railway type, and such features at the ends of the avenues of our modern cities suggest a great terminal even to a stranger when seen for the first time."[63]

McKim split apart the distinguishing features of the shed. He used the traditional vocabulary of glass and steel over the train concourse, and he transferred the shed's tall arches to the waiting hall. On the interior, these arches read as thermal windows, fitting for an ancient bath (see Fig. 1.52). On the exterior, they signified a train station. The architects explained: "The General Waiting Room, with its semicircular shaped windows of unusual dimensions was in reality created in order to give to the exterior of the building a suggestion of familiar type of form when seen from a distance. The view, for instance, of the station when looking down 32nd Street from Fourth, Fifth and Sixth Avenues (Fig. 1.58) would seem to us to suggest a railway type such as, for instance, the Gare de l'Est in Paris."[64] The elevated profile of the waiting hall was essential to the station's urban identity, making it recognizable from afar.[65] McKim did not anticipate the negative impact as skyscrapers encroached on Penn Station, cutting off views from the avenues and undermining the urban impact of the waiting hall.

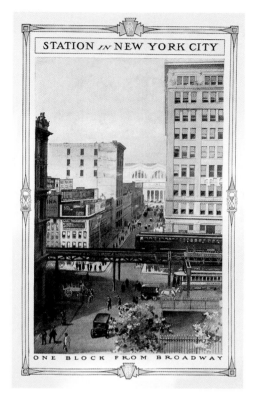

Big as the waiting hall was, it was not the climax of the journey. The procession through Penn Station culminated in the concourse, one of the great spaces of American architecture (Figs. 1.59 and 1.60). The concourse was essentially a courtyard enclosed by stone-clad walls and a canopy of glazed vaults supported on steel columns. Where the waiting

1.60. Train concourse facing south, 1910. Photograph by De W. C. Ward.

hall felt weighty, the concourse was skeletal and diaphanous. Compared to the soaring vault of the waiting hall, the concourse vault was low; the height dropped from 150 to 90 feet from one room to the next. The spatial compression directed attention down to the tracks, which were illuminated by natural light and visible through the cut-away floor The vista of sky above and tracks below created a sense of transparency in the concourse, as if the visitor was seeing with x-ray vision.

The procession through the station was designed to propel travelers to this point, where the forward motion of arriving passengers was connected to the movement of the trains. Yet the room was not strongly directed. Rather it created a matrix of contrasting forces: trains slipped in and out on one axis, the vaults were oriented the other way, and crowds hovered in between. Added to this was the slow-motion parade of the sun and clouds that filtered through the transparent vaults. Orchestrating movements that varied in direction, pattern, and tempo, the train concourse distilled motion so that it could be observed before setting it free.

McKim carefully selected building materials, attuned to color, texture, the play of light, and tectonic meaning. He employed pink granite, his favorite stone, for the exterior of Penn Station because of its color and durability. He chose travertine, the stone of ancient Rome, for the arcade and waiting hall. Grand but practical, travertine was easy to maintain, had a "warm, sunny color," and "tended to take a polish, and improve by contact and use rather than to absorb dirt." For the floor of the concourse and the exterior sidewalks he chose glass block in order to let natural light filter down to track level.[66]

1.61. Interior view of the train station in Frankfurt, Germany from an album of Charles McKim.

McKim paid equal attention to the exposed steel in the concourse (see Figs. 1.59 and 1.60). Because the concourse was constructed in steel and glass, it is often characterized as a strictly functional design, in contrast to the classical, masonry-clad waiting hall. This interpretation sees the adjacent spaces in oppositional terms: classical versus modern, masonry versus steel, ornament versus structure, rhetoric versus function. This interpretation, I believe, is wrong because it ignores the refined design of the concourse and fails to probe its meaning. McKim did not construct an opposition but rather a continuum by translating the classical language of the waiting hall into forms suitable for steel. Lewis Mumford once remarked that "the gap between stone and steel-and-glass was as great as that in the evolutionary order between the crustaceans and vertebrates."[67] McKim took the opposite view and tried to close the gap. There is no denying his anxiety about the changing world, but it did not stifle McKim's creativity at Penn Station. Rather he answered the conservative challenge with a powerful demonstration of the relevance of historical building forms in modern times.

McKim regarded the steel frame of the concourse as a problem of design no less than engineering. He admired the beautifully designed structural features of European train stations, and his railroad album documents a special interest in the magnificent train shed in Frankfurt (Fig. 1.61). "We have attempted (I believe for the first time in this country)," Richardson explained, "to give to purely structural steel an adequate architectural expres-

1.62. Train concourse facing northeast showing the Guastavino domes during construction, September 11, 1909. Photograph by Louis Dreyer.

sion without making any material sacrifice of structural efficiency of design to arbitrary aesthetic requirements. It has always seemed to us [McKim, Mead & White] that while the average structural steel turned out in this country is admirably adapted for its purpose from the point of view of stability, and also well designed from the standpoint of economical fabrication in the mills, the question of its structural appearance when erected has frequently been neglected to an unfortunate degree." [68] Exactly how McKim determined the shape of the vaults and guided the structural engineers, Westinghouse Church Kerr & Company, is set forth in an account of the design process, probably written by Richardson.

> The main architectural lines were first determined, namely the location of the columns, arches and domes, and the general height and breadth of the intersecting members, the steel engineer being then given the problem of designing a structure which would conform to the architectural lines outlined, the detail being a question

of co-operation and adjustment from both points of view. The type and scale of the lattice work, as well as the lines and sizes of the arches, notably the variation in depth between the spring and top lines of the arches, as well as varying widths between the diagonal ribs and the vault lines, was suggested to the engineer to obtain a variety of effect and to avoid the monotony which would result in the assembling of arches of similar forms and dimensions. [69]

The architects purposely rejected the wide-span barrel vault of a standard train shed in favor of a variety of vaults.[70] Three groin vaults cover the main floor area, where passengers stand before descending to the tracks. They are aligned with the groin vaults of the waiting hall, whose underlying steel structure they lay bare. Two rows of narrow barrel vaults demarcate the area above the tracks, and a row of Guastavino domes with glazed oculi line the perimeter of the concourse on three sides (all but the east side, where the waiting hall is located) (Fig. 1.62). Unlike the groin and barrel vaults, which are entirely glazed, the Guastavino domes are a masonry shell—that is, they combine the two tectonic systems of the station, masonry and steel.

Structural simplicity was sacrificed in order to fulfill architectural goals because McKim's complex design of the concourse vault prevented an economical engineering solution. The engineers had to make two significant compromises. First, compared to what was required to cover the concourse by a standard truss, like the truss over the baggage courtyards (Fig. 1.63), McKim's design demanded an excessive use of steel, which meant the structure was unnecessarily heavy and costly. Second, the steel engineers originally proposed to stabilize the arches with tie bars, but the architects found the visual effect of horizontal ties unacceptable and rejected this structural solution. As a result, the engineers designed a system with a more expensive cantilever type arch, that is a bent steel beam cantilevered from the surrounding structure. A network of webbed trusses created the effect of barrel vaults below, and the groin vaults were suspended from diagonal trusses forming a pyramidal pattern in the roof.[71] An exterior view of the concourse roof gives a clearer picture of the actual structure than an interior view into the canopy

1.63. The north baggage courtyard and skylight, 1910. Photograph by De W.C. Ward.

PENNSYLVANIA STATION
of
P. T. & T. R. R.
ROOF CONCOURSE
FEB. 18TH 1910.

L. H. DREYER, PHOTO.

1.64. The roof of the train concourse looking northwest, February 18, 1910. The Main Signal Cabin station is visible in the track yard, at the top left. Photograph by Louis Dreyer.

of vaults, which created the illusion of replicating a masonry vault in steel (Fig. 1.64). The concourse beautifully represents an idea about structure—that stone and steel are analogous and speak a common language because they can be given the same arched shaped. But this idea was false and did not correspond with the actual structure of the station, which was masked both in the waiting hall and the concourse.

Richardson related the use of exposed steel to the practical function of the concourse. "In addition to the arbitrary design of the architects to give to the structural steel a dignified expression . . . , there was also the idea of obtaining an appropriate transition between the purely architectural lines of the General Waiting Room and adjoining rooms of the building and the railway and engineering operations features adjacent so that one would be led from the more monumental side of the Station to the utilitarian by an easy and conscious gradation of effect."[72] His point, of course, is valid, but also incomplete because it fails to explain the system of the vaults and the use of mixed-media Guastavino domes, which crystallize McKim's effort to reconcile masonry and steel. The vaults throughout the station establish a relationship between two building systems, which are made to echo each other, interpenetrate, and speak a common language.

Note also the elegant, elongated shape of the latticed steel columns. At the springing point of the arches, a kind of capital appears; what was originally a simple molding in Crow's renderings (Fig. 1.65) has blossomed into a fully developed capital with lamps projecting from all four sides (see Figs. 1.59 and 1.60). The lighting fixtures unify function and ornament and convert the steel columns into a modern order.

One final detail confirms McKim's interest in combining masonry and steel construction. An early rendering of the commercial arcade calls for both large and small pilasters made of stone (Fig. 1.66). However, the design was changed so that the minor order and shop fronts were built of cast iron (see Figs. 1.49 and 1.50). The revision may appear minor, but it systematically extends the design logic. McKim's intention was to forge an alliance between masonry and steel, classical forms and modern structures, historic building types and modern needs. Simply put, Pennsylvania Station made the history of architecture relevant to the conditions of twentieth-century urban life.

MODERN CONVENIENCE

Pennsylvania Station was built on the threshold of a revolution in architecture. Within a decade, modernists championed a new value system based on a streamlined machine aesthetic, functionalism, and structural expression. From this perspective, Penn Station appeared irredeemably old-fashioned. The new critical establishment had little appreciation for McKim's refined use of the orders, which progressed from Doric on the exterior to Ionic in the commercial arcade and Corinthian in the waiting hall. It failed to notice, let alone admire, the new order in the concourse designed for latticed steel and lightbulbs.

1.65. An early project for the train concourse, c.1905–6. Rendering by Jules Crow.

1.66. An early project for the commercial arcade, c.1905–6. Rendering by Jules Crow.

1.67. 33rd Street driveway and pedestrian bridge facing Seventh Avenue, 1910. Photograph by De W. C. Ward.

opposite

1.68. Plan at the level of the exit concourse of Pennsylvania Station.

1.69. Exit concourse, 1910. The glass-block floor of the train concourse and sidewalks admitted light to the lower levels of the station. Photograph by De W. C. Ward.

Critics also faulted the station for a false image of structure, since the masonry walls and coffered vaults masked a steel frame, while incorrectly assuming that the exposed steel vaults of the train concourse revealed the true structure. This perspective tended to obscure other modern features of the station, features that enhanced the convenience of passengers and enabled the station to function efficiently. Forget the style of the building. In terms of function, Pennsylvania Station was a thoroughly modern facility.

First and foremost, the station was designed to facilitate circulation under highly congested conditions. "Movement is the essence of transportation," Lewis Mumford observed, "and movement is what McKim's plan magnificently provided for."[73] Given the monumentality of the building, it was surprisingly porous, with multiple entrances on all sides—ten different entrances above ground plus underground connections to subways.[74] In order to channel thousands of passengers to eleven different platforms without facing the rush of traffic moving in the opposite direction, Penn Station undertook a pioneering experiment in traffic control by differentiating traffic streams—chauffeur-driven from pedestrian, incoming from outgoing, long-distance from commuter. Vehicles entered by internal driveways, twice as wide as the outside street, that sloped down to the train concourse level. The 31st Street driveway was for embarking passengers, the 33rd Street one for those disembarking (Fig. 1.67). Pedestrian bridges over the driveways led directly to the waiting hall.

Exiting passengers bypassed the train concourse, which was crowded with those waiting to board trains. Stairs led from the train platforms to an exit concourse and from there to outlets to the surrounding streets (Figs. 1.68 and 1.69). Set eighteen feet above the tracks, the exit concourse was designed to be level with future subway entrances so as to facilitate transit connections. Richardson hailed the exit concourse as an innovation, "the first instance in America of any serious attempt at such a division of traffic, and there not as in Europe, to different sides of the station, but to different levels."[75] The multi-tiered street systems envisioned in the 1920s by Hugh Ferriss, Harvey Wiley Corbett, and Ernest Flagg, among other urban reformers, as a way of decongesting the streets of Manhattan may well have drawn upon their experience of the circulation system of Penn Station.

One entrance was unusual because it was a block away. In order to obtain an outlet on 34th Street, the Pennsylvania Railroad acquired a swath of land north of the station, from

33rd to 34th Streets. It was the only land the company bought for reasons other than railroad operations (i.e., to build tracks, tunnels, or the generating station). The initial idea was to build a covered passageway on the axis of the waiting hall, with a stepped ramp descending from 34th Street to the two concourse levels below grade. McKim's model was the ramp leading to the Campidoglio in Rome.[76] When it became clear that the station would not have subway service in the near future, railroad officials deemed it necessary to enlarge the 34th Street entrance and make a full-fledged street in the middle of the block. McKim, Mead & White endorsed this approach in a letter to Rea in December 1908:

As the construction of the station progresses, we feel more keenly than ever the need of adequate approaches to a building of such monumental importance, both from the artistic and practical point of view. It has become apparent, even to the layman, that the approach from Sixth Avenue through 32nd Street is far too narrow, and we have noted that it is becoming a matter of popular regret that the property in front of the station between Sixth and Seventh Avenue will inevitably be filled up with lofty buildings practically hiding much of the station from view from the main arteries of the city. With a street from 34th Street, leading directly to the General Waiting Room, you will have two approaches on main axes, and if such a street were made the same width as 34th Street,

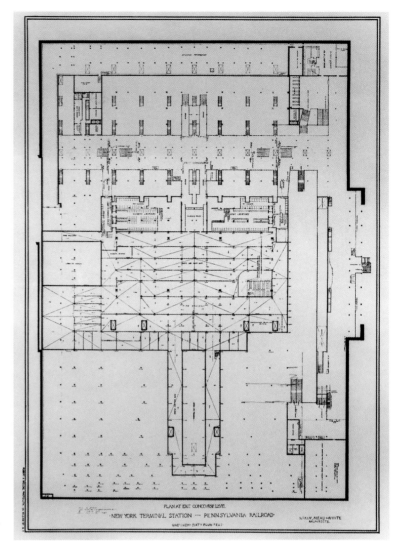

namely 100 feet wide, the adjoining property, having such a splendid frontage, would become very valuable, and in addition, it might be found practicable for the New York City Railway Company to turn their 34th Street car tracks through this proposed street as far as 33rd Street, thus bringing 34th Street to your station instead of trying to bring your station to 34th Street. [77]

The railroad cleared a walkway 80 feet wide, somewhat narrower than the architects had recommended.[78] Stairs and an escalator extended from the two concourses to 34th Street, where the opening in the ground was simply fenced, and the private street was otherwise paved and planted. But these were only short-term measures. "It would seem that some building development must occur in this property within a short time after the Station is opened, and therefore any expenditure which we put in at this point beyond the actual necessities would be a waste of money," Gibbs wrote Rea.[79] The subsequent development of the private street is discussed in the section on the neighborhood below.

Another aspect of efficient circulation was reducing the distance from the station entrances to the trains. The pressure to shorten this distance was complicated at Penn Station by the significant vertical drop from the street level to the tracks. According to a study by George Gibbs, chief engineer of the station, the vertical distance from street level to train platform was significantly greater at Penn Station than in other forms of transit in New York City. At Penn Station the vertical distance ranged from 36 to 42 feet, depending on the street entrance (the site sloped down to the west)—substantially more than the climb of 23 feet at the 42nd Street station of the IRT subway, 23 feet (on average) for the Ninth Avenue elevated railroad line, and 25 feet (on average) for the Sixth Avenue elevated. Even at Grand Central Terminal, where the tracks were on two levels, the climb was less onerous: 39 feet for suburban passengers at the lower level, and only 17 feet for long-distance travelers on the upper level. "Our climb," Gibbs wrote, "is very much more than the people are in the habit of making, either in the subway or elevated. . . . Anything which can be reasonably done to cut down this physical exertion and loss of time should be given our best consideration."[80]

In order to make the level change comfortable to negotiate on foot, McKim created a horizontal sequence of unfolding spaces that descend from east to west by way of stairs, except for the driveways, which were sloped. The waiting hall and train concourse are midway in the descent, 20 feet below street level. Given the horizontal extension of Penn Station, McKim's achievement in designing efficient circulation paths is impressive. According to data assembled by Richardson, the distance from street to track at Burnham's Union Station was 1,200 feet; at Grand Central Terminal, 1,100 feet; and at Penn Station, 980 feet from Seventh Avenue, and 480 feet from the side entrances.[81]

McKim's job was to balance two competing goals — to reduce the impact of the vertical drop yet compress the distance between the two end points, a job he solved elegantly.

The station had an extraordinary range of amenities. The baggage system, for example, was one of the most advanced in the world; it removed baggage from passenger platforms, where it was typically stacked and sorted, and kept it out of sight until the train journey ended. Passengers could check luggage in the driveways or the waiting hall. It was sorted in the main baggage room below the commercial arcade and lowered by hydraulic lift to corridors twenty feet below the tracks where electric trucks distributed baggage to the proper car and platform.[82] Other amenities included shops in the commercial arcade, single-sex waiting rooms and smoking rooms, a dining room and lunch counter, vending machines, well-maintained pay toilets, barber shop, private rooms for funeral parties, and no less than 158 cooled water fountains (Fig. 1.70). Railroad employees had their own YMCA facilities with gym, bowling alley, lecture rooms, and assembly

1.70. Barber shop, 1910. Photograph by De W. C. Ward.

1.71. Power house on 31st Street, 1910. Photograph by De W. C. Ward.

hall, located in the Eighth Avenue wing. The omnipresent clocks, synchronized with the U.S. Naval Observatory by a master timepiece in the dispatcher's office, were not only an element of utility but also a major feature of the decoration. A 6-foot clock was the centerpiece of the sculptural grouping on the street facades, a 15-foot clock in the waiting hall was the focal point of the long vista from the main entrance, and 10-foot clocks hung above the entrances to the concourse (see Figs. 1.42, 1.53, and 1.60).[83]

Beyond the electric cars required for the New York tunnels, Penn Station precipitated other improvements in railroad service and rolling stock. It introduced the use of raised platforms in the United States. An early rendering of the tracks shows the original intention to use the standard low platform, at track level (see Fig. 1. 65). The Pennsylvania Railroad raised the platforms to the level of the train cars, as was customary in England.

1.72. Project for Grand Central
Terminal by Stanford White,
1903.

The change eliminated about seven vertical feet from the climb to the concourse and shaved a minute off a passenger's unloading time.[84] The railroad also overhauled passenger cars to eliminate the risk of fire in the tunnels. A new line of all-steel cars was commissioned, although Rea would not publicize this improvement for fear that the railroad's safety concerns would alarm the public. "As our Company now fully realizes the advantages of steel cars, further publications connecting the necessity for these cars with the New York tunnel is not desirable, because of the idea which might become prevalent that we expect to have fires in the tunnel."[85]

A generating station on 31st Street built across from the station, also to designs by McKim, Mead & White, met the intensive power needs of this miniature city (Fig. 1.71). (The building still stands.) The electrical current used by the Pennsylvania and LIRR trains was generated by a different power plant on the east bank of the East River, at Hunter's Point, erected in 1903, when the New York extension was launched.[86]

CROSSTOWN RIVALRY

Alexander Cassatt, president of the Pennsylvania Railroad, was an enlightened client but also a shrewd businessman. He built Pennsylvania Station because it was necessary for the Pennsylvania Railroad Company's continued growth and its effectiveness in competing with the New York Central. In terms of Manhattan-bound traffic, New York Central had a significant advantage: a station in New York—Grand Central Terminal, originally opened on 42nd Street and Fourth Avenue in 1871. The New York Central had resolved to electrify the lines servicing Grand Central in 1899–1900, before the Pennsylvania's New York extension was launched, but the Pennsylvania's ambitious plans provoked a response. In December 1902, eight months after McKim was commissioned to design Pennsylvania Station, the New York Central dropped its plans to remodel Grand Central Terminal and decided to build a new station. The New York Central announced a closed architectural competition on January 15, 1903 and invited four firms, including McKim, Mead & White, to submit designs by March 1.

With McKim involved with Penn Station, Stanford White took charge of the competition project for Grand Central. One can only imagine the atmosphere in the office of McKim, Mead & White with the two principal design partners at work on rival train stations. White had only six weeks to design a complex building. It is reasonable to suppose some consultation with McKim, who had a considerable headstart in thinking about a parallel project, but whatever may have transpired in the office, White took the opposite approach to his partner's. McKim had championed the idea of a freestanding monument and prevailed upon Cassatt to abandon the idea of building a hotel above Penn Station. White, on the other hand, embraced this idea and submerged his station in a hotel and office complex. In two slightly different schemes for Grand Central Terminal, White proposed a fourteen-story rectangular block with corner towers and a sixty-story skyscraper, which would have been the tallest building in New York City (Fig. 1.72). Although William H. Newman, president of the New York Central, found White's solution "far too extensive and impracticable," he favored the concept of a revenue-producing building above the station.[87] The winning scheme by Reed & Stem that Newman selected included a twenty-story hotel over the headhouse.

Newman was looking at the bottom line, but William K. Vanderbilt, chairman of the New York Central, had his eye on Penn Station. In 1904, after McKim's designs were published, Vanderbilt intervened in the design process and instructed the architects to eliminate the hotel. Demanding a freestanding monument, Vanderbilt had no intention of allowing a crosstown rival to eclipse the grandeur of Grand Central. In short, the decision not to build above Penn Station spurred the owners of Grand Central to do the same. Bridge designer Gustav Lindenthal acknowledged this productive rivalry in a letter to Rea: "Everyone concedes that the Pennsylvania Railroad has been at extraordinary pains to make its railroad station in this city architecturally beautiful, and that fact may be said to have induced the New York Central Railroad to go to the very large expense of a new terminal building for its own road, conceived also on monumental lines."[88] The remarkably rich materials used in Grand Central—Stoney Creek granite and Bedford limestone on the exterior, Bottocino marble and Caen limestone on the interior—reflects the same rivalrous impulse.

The design of Penn Station was finalized well before that of Grand Central, which was not resolved until 1910. The design process was turbulent because in 1904 Vanderbilt forced Reed & Stem to collaborate with the rival firm of Warren and Wetmore, which was determined to undo the winning scheme. Over the next six years, the hostile firms repeatedly changed the design. By the time a compromise was forged and construction began in 1910, Penn Station was completed. Thus the Grand Central architects, when they were not bickering, had ample opportunity to study McKim's design and take cues from it. Certain pioneering features of Penn Station, such as multiple entrances, the multilevel circulation system, and especially ramps, were used more extensively and with greater success at Grand Central.

While the two stations shared a similar preoccupation with efficient circulation and decongestion, their plans differ in a fundamental respect. The layout of Grand Central did not privilege any particular approach. The numerous pathways to the main concourse are treated more or less equally. Penn Station, on the other hand, emphasized the pathway extending from the central portico on Seventh Avenue. The architectural experience of the station was oriented to only one subset of travelers: passengers arriving at this particular entrance. Those entering elsewhere in the station might enjoy a part of the architectural procession, but not passengers disembarking from trains, about half the public using the station. Disembarking passengers were mostly expected to exit from the station by other routes.

McKim described Penn Station as a monumental gateway, yet it primarily played that

1.73. An early project for Pennsylvania Station and the Post Office, c.1905–6. Rendering by Jules Crow.

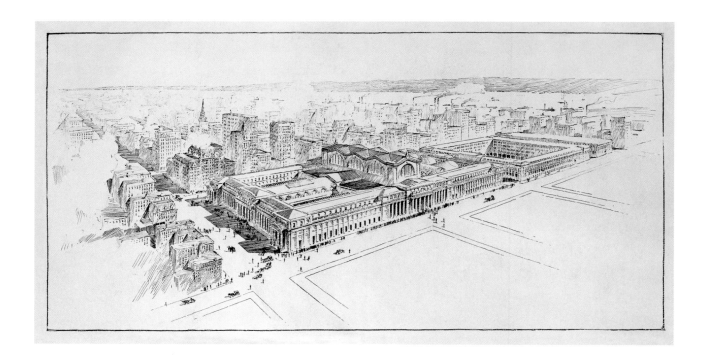

role in one direction. Where the plan of Grand Central was informal and democratic, the plan of Penn Station was ceremonial and hierarchical. These qualities did not impair the functionality of Penn Station, which was a highly porous structure with numerous entrances, as we have seen, but the plan reveals a tension McKim was unable to resolve fully, a tension between the architectural value of ceremony and grandeur to which he was committed and the modern necessity for efficiency which the proper function of a train station required. Grand Central Terminal reordered these priorities: ceremony was subordinated to efficiency.

THE RAILROAD'S URBAN VISION

Rea was disturbed. "The New York Central are proceeding in a very large way to develop their property alongside and overhead their tracks at the Grand Central Terminal and have created a new centre, and why should our Company, with its superior credit, sit still and see many other sections of New York City developed to the detriment of our Pennsylvania Station neighborhood?"[89] The date was March 1912; the new Grand Central Terminal was not even open. Yet it was already evident that Grand Central was playing a more important urbanistic role than Pennsylvania Station. What went wrong around Penn Station?

1.74. Plan of the environs of Pennsylvania Station, showing the proposed mid-block private streets connecting to 30th and 34th Streets, c.1909.

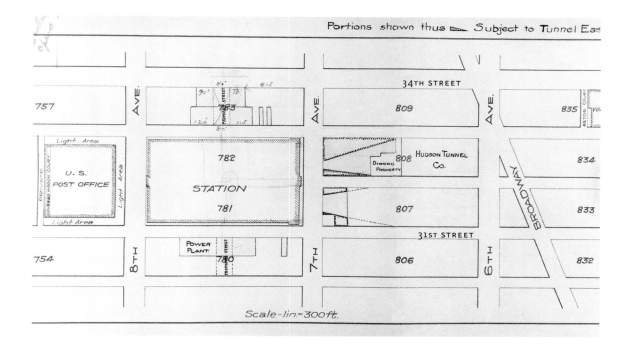

It was not that the railroad lacked an urban vision. The Pennsylvania Railroad had a plan to develop the station's environs. It is partially illustrated in two drawings by Jules Crow from 1905–6, but the full scope of the company's vision is only revealed in Rea's correspondence. The overall strategy was to reinforce the architectural character of the station with harmoniously designed buildings on adjacent sites and to increase access from local streets, specifically from 34th Street by opening a private, midblock street and from Herald Square by widening 32nd Street (Figs. 1.73 and 1.74). Rea elaborated the railroad's goals in a letter to the Municipal Art Society in 1910.

In view of the rather cheap character of the property adjacent to our Station, this section of the City could be very much beautified by an architectural treatment of the entire surroundings, and the territory between Broadway and the Station, and Twenty-third and Forty-second Streets, enlarged by new streets and traffic facilities to ease congestion. . . . Further, while not a necessity from our Company's standpoint, we believed that much more might be done for this central section of the City adjoining Broadway, if an additional street should exist as a continuation of said private way between Seventh and Eighth Avenues, from 34th to 42nd Streets, and further, a similar treatment might occur between 31st and 23rd Streets. Little has been done for this section of the City and this suggested street through these long blocks of the property would be an additional safeguard in case of fire, would beautify this part of the City, which badly needs improvement, and would make another avenue for the quick carriage of traffic up and downtown in these busy sections.[90]

A new north-south avenue running, in effect, through the waiting hall of Pennsylvania Station and subdividing the wide blocks of the West Side was a fine idea.[91] So was another proposal endorsed by the Pennsylvania Railroad for a diagonal boulevard and underground trolley line connecting Penn Station with Grand Central Terminal, a scheme promoted by the Architectural League in 1911–12.[92] Rea wrote municipal officials on behalf of the new streets, but he understood that real estate values militated against ambitious street plans. In any event, to improve access to the station, the railroad pinned its hopes on an even more ambitious plan—the subway.

At the time it launched the New York extension, the Pennsylvania Railroad believed construction would begin imminently on a Seventh or Eighth Avenue subway line. The station was designed with those connections in mind, not as a far-off, theoretical possibility, but as a short-term reality. The connections are a prominent feature of the architectural model of the station made in 1904 and displayed at the St. Louis World's Fair (see Fig. 1.21). But the intricate politics of subway construction in New York City proved that the early optimism of Pennsylvania officials was naive. In 1905 the Rapid Transit Commission laid out a plan for nineteen new subway routes, including four lines that would have served Penn Station: a southern extension of the IRT line from Times Square to the Battery, plus lines on Eighth and Ninth Avenues and 34th Street. However, this plan did not lead to construction, and the next plan, released in 1908 (the Triborough plan) did not so much as touch the West Side of Manhattan. Behind the scenes, the railroad lobbied municipal officials for a subway link to Penn Station, but the city appeared indifferent to the Pennsylvania's concerns. The Seventh Avenue line was approved in 1913, but the line was not fully operational until 1918 (shuttle service between Times Square and Penn Station began in June 1917). Penn Station had a long wait for its first subway connection, and an even longer one for the next. The Eighth Avenue line opened in 1932.

The absence of subway service had a profound impact on Penn Station. First, it undermined the efficiency of McKim's plan. The distance from the point of entry to the trains was relatively short, especially for passengers who arrived by car, but the majority of travelers relied on public transit. It was not such a long walk to the streetcars on 34th Street—only 710 feet—thanks to the private midblock street, nor to streetcars on Seventh and Eighth Avenues, 940 and 525 feet away, respectively. But to get to the transit lines at Herald Square, the preferred lines because they served the city's shopping districts, was a trek of 1,600 feet.[93] The distances to transit connections at Grand Central were considerably shorter because the station was on the original IRT subway line. More importantly from an urban perspective, the lack of subway service depressed development of the neighborhood around Penn Station. It impeded access to the West Side blocks, curtailed pedestrian traffic, and kept land values down. Although streetcar lines served the area, they were inefficient forms of transportation compared to the subway and could not compete as agents of urban growth. The inauguration of the first subway in 1904 created dynamic new centers, notably Times Square and the Grand Central area, while Penn Station was cut off from this urban lifeline, at least at a formative time.

The subway was only a part of the problem. As one developer explained to Rea, "It is not a question of more transportation facilities (though these are always helpful) as much as the purifying of the neighborhood by the occupancy of the streets by respectable people doing business or living in hotels there."[94] The railroad's actions to reform the neighborhood, populate the streets, and promote passenger traffic were also important. Unquestionably, the railroad did not do enough. It was hampered by a limited urban vision that focused on coordinated ensembles and regulated facades. McKim paid more attention to formal elements than to the kinds of activities and uses that should be encouraged around the station. Moreover, the formal ingredients of his plan—long, uniform facades, porticoes, plazas, and wide setbacks—were ill suited to the context in

1.75. The west facade of the U.S. Post Office looking east over the railyard before construction of the annex, November 28, 1932.

1.76. U.S. Post Office from the corner of 31st Street and Eighth Avenue, September 4, 1912.

Manhattan, in terms of both its street grid and its real estate market. The shortcomings of McKim's urban vision were not, however, responsible for the Pennsylvania Railroad's cautious attitude toward real estate development, which was a critical factor.

THE RAILROAD AS REAL ESTATE DEVELOPER

The first, and only, piece of the Pennsylvania's plan to fall into place quickly was the Post Office on Eighth Avenue, which can be seen in an early rendering of the improved neighborhood (see Fig. 1.73). In June 1906, the U.S. government bought the air rights west of the station for $1.66 million; the railroad retained ownership of the underlying tracks. The Pennsylvania Railroad transported a little more than 40 percent of New York's outgoing mail; the daily total, including incoming mail, amounted to 200 tons of letters to be sorted—hence the logic of building a post office directly over the tracks (Fig. 1.75). Equipped with a system of conveyor belts, the Post Office was able to move mail between the platforms and sorting rooms in record time. It worried Rea that the federal competition for the Post Office failed to specify that the design should harmonize with Penn Station. Nevertheless, the jury selected McKim, Mead & White in 1908, and the federal government allowed Penn Station to define the character of its building. Construction began in

1.78. A project for the 32nd Street approach to Pennsylvania Station, 1906. Rendering by Jules Crow. Of the original suite of thirteen renderings by Crow, this is the only drawing to survive; the others are documented in photographs and glass slides.

1909, and the Post Office opened in 1913 (Fig. 1.76).[95]

Rea's willingness to sell the air rights to the Ninth Avenue frontage encountered opposition.[96] Engineer Gibbs argued that construction over the tracks would add obstructing columns to the railyard and interfere with the efficient movement of trains, concerns eventually disproved when the Post Office Annex was built in 1935 (Fig. 1.77).[97] In any event, the more powerful and long-term obstacle to air-rights development came not from railroad men but from realtors, who showed no interest in this far western patch of New York City. It is not that the Pennsylvania Railroad ignored the possibility of air-rights development, a charge sometimes made in comparisons with the New York Central, which sold air rights on an eight-block stretch of Park Avenue. The Pennsylvania was constrained by the geography of its western approach to Manhattan. Its tracks landed on the far west side, a remote, and therefore uncommercial, location, unlike Park Avenue.

With good reason, Rea was more concerned about the east side of the station, where shopping and public transit were a block away. McKim designed a classical scheme for the main approach, consisting of a plaza in front of the station on Seventh Avenue; an enlargement of 32nd Street between Broadway and the station; and dignified, porticoed buildings along 32nd Street (Fig. 1.78). The railroad owned some but not all of the properties affected by this design. Because of high land costs, it had bought only what was needed to build the cross-town tunnels under 32nd and 33rd Streets. It owned most of the Seventh Avenue frontage between 31st and 33rd Streets, but not the corner lot on 31st Street and not much of 32nd Street. "My reason for desiring control of all this frontage—31st to 33rd Streets," Rea explained in 1908 to Henry Frick, a director of the Pennsylvania Railroad, "is to control the character of the structure, keeping it in accord with our station, and, if possible, arrange for setting back twenty or twenty-five feet so as to have a widened avenue in front of our station. . . . In my judgment we should secure this plaza even if we are unable to procure anything from the city for the property thrown into the Street, because of its great advantage to our Station Building."[98] McKim set the station back 20 feet from the building line on Seventh Avenue and proposed pulling the curbline back as well, in that way widening the avenue and providing half the space needed for a plaza.

The plaza scheme hinged on the Pennsylvania Railroad's purchase of one additional lot, the empty corner of Seventh Avenue and 31st Street (see Fig. 1.74). The owners were asking $230,000 for the property. The Pennsylvania received an appraisal of $197,500, based on what the railroad had paid for neighboring properties. The difference was $32,500, a nominal amount, and Rea requested permission from James McCrea, Cassatt's successor as president of the Pennsylvania Railroad, to buy the property.[99] McCrea opposed further investment in New York real estate. Four years later, in 1912, William Mead, of McKim, Mead & White, wrote his partner Richardson about the persistent corner problem. "Your proposition of setting the new Pennsylvania Buildings on [the east side of] Seventh Avenue back 15 feet seems to me to have one very serious objection, and that is, if they don't own the property on the south corner that owner would have a perfect right to bring his building, and probably would, out to the line. What work of composition would that make? It seems to me as if the Pennsylvania Company must have that property."[100] The railroad came to a different conclusion. It would not pay even the relatively modest amount demanded for the corner lot, and thus the plaza was doomed. A short time later, a four-story brick hotel for men only was built on the northeast corner of Seventh Avenue and 31st Street, exactly the kind of building that the railroad expected rising land values to eliminate.

Likewise, the 32nd Street renovation project was doomed because the railroad did not control the land. The biggest landowner was the Hudson Companies, the realty company of the Hudson and Manhattan Railroad Company, which owned a large property on Sixth Avenue between 32nd and 33rd Streets. In March 1909 the Hudson Companies announced an agreement to build a department store for Gimbel Brothers, who signed a long-term lease. Gimbel's agreed to an arcaded facade along 32nd Street, but opposed the 10-foot setback required to make the street 80 feet wide. When the owners on the south side of 32nd Street took the reverse position—against the arcades and for the setback—another one of McKim's ideas was killed.[101] Voluntary compliance was not a good way to realize an expensive architectural scheme.

While the Seventh Avenue plaza and the 32nd Street project were thwarted because the railroad did not own the land, the railroad faced another set of problems on land it did own. In determining what to do with its property on Seventh Avenue opposite the station, Rea grappled with two basic issues: when to develop the land, and how it should be done. Rea initially wanted to develop the property as quickly as possible because an improvement would benefit the station; a hotel, for example, "would tend to bring us more traffic, would clean up the whole situation, [and] would add additional value to other property of which we have a large amount to sell or lease. . . ." On the other hand, property values remained low in 1908. The railroad had acquired the area between 32nd and 33rd Streets on Seventh Avenue for $32.42 per square foot in 1903. In 1908 it was appraised at $33.15 per square foot by one realtor and $29 by another, who said the tunnel easement on the land adversely affected its value. Values were expected to rise after the station opened, thus as Rea saw it, "profit would accrue by waiting."[102] Since no offers met Rea's threshold price of $40 per square foot, the railroad postponed action in anticipation of an upturn once trains were rolling into the station.

The other question was what role the railroad should play in the development process. It could sell the land and step away from all continuing obligations. It could rent an improvement leasehold and retain ownership of the underlying land. Or it could play a more active role in developing the site, beginning with financing construction. In 1908 Rea, like most of his colleagues at the Pennsylvania Railroad, did not think the company should invest additional capital in real estate activities. As he put it in a letter to the president of the Hudson Companies, "We have taken the position all along that our first duty was to provide a railroad station with every facility conceivable to be necessary or desirable for our patrons, and if after that we had rentable space well and good."[103] As Rea learned about New York real estate, however, he began to change his mind. By 1910 he thought the railroad should finance the improvement on Seventh Avenue and urged the Pennsylvania's real estate committee to follow the example of the Hudson Companies, which built the Gimbel store.

The traditional railroad priorities of the Pennsylvania conflicted with Rea's suggested approach. In 1911 the Special Committee on New York Surplus Property decided "that they were going to exhaust their efforts to sell the property." If and only if this approach failed, "they might consider building a hotel and leasing, but until that time they are not willing to take up and consider any of the propositions which would contemplate our Company raising money of the use of its credit."[104] President McCrea endorsed the sale of New York properties not used for railroad purposes. The authorized selling price of the Seventh Avenue property was $4.2 million ($3 million for the property north of 32nd Street, $1.2 million for the smaller lot to the south). The assessed value of the property was $3,294,000, which meant that the company was willing to accept a paper profit of $900,000. In 1911 the real estate market was declining, and the railroad could not get its asking price.[105]

Absent any buyers, Rea pursued his aim of leasing the land between 32nd and 33rd Streets to Gimbel's. The possibility of one large department store covering the entire block was considered briefly before the railroad offered to build a separate store on its property and lease it to Gimbel's on the same terms offered by the Hudson Companies. Railroad officials eagerly anticipated passageways through the department store connecting Penn Station to the transit lines serving Herald Square: the Sixth Avenue elevated and the Hudson and Manhattan line, which had a terminal beneath Gimbel's. In order to facilitate this development, the Pennsylvania Railroad spent $1 million in 1912 to buy an adjoining property on the north side of 32nd Street, which squared off its property. The west half of the block between Sixth and Seventh Avenues was now fully controlled by the railroad, and the east half by the Hudson Companies.[106] The purchase was inconsistent with the railroad's prior stance. Evidently the prospective deal with Gimbel's encouraged the railroad to pursue a more aggressive approach. It was sorely disappointed in 1912 when, after almost two years of negotiations, the deal collapsed because Gimbel Brothers chose not to expand.[107]

By this time, it was not only the Pennsylvania Railroad that was unhappy about its unproductive real estate but all of New York City as well. Newspapers roundly criticized the failure of Penn Station to upgrade its neighborhood. "Is the Pennsylvania Station a Failure? Real Estate Brokers Say It Has Not Aided the Growth of the Section," read a headline in the New York *Sun* in 1912.[108] Cheap businesses had not turned into first-class retail. Arriving passengers "take cars and escape almost as if the station were in a plague spot."[109] A developer with interests north of Penn Station complained to Rea in a letter typical of many in his files. "I find my endeavors thwarted at every step by the constant opposition of my [real estate] clients, because of your apathy as compared with the zeal and activity of the New York Central people."[110]

Stung by repeated criticism, Rea began to collect information about the New York Central's development activities. He clipped newspaper articles on the subject and made inquiries about the way it structured deals, managed air rights, and amortized the investment in Grand Central Terminal. Rea contacted his counterparts directly. He wrote the president of the New York, New Haven and Hudson River Railroad Company, in June 1913, to ask about the railroad's new building on Vanderbilt Avenue and 45th Street: "We have some similar leases to make and I thought I would like to compare them with yours."[111] The comparative data Rea collected was revealing. It showed that in 1909 real estate around Grand Central hovered at $50 to $60 per square foot, with $75 at the high end (for the Hotel Belmont site), while the land around Penn Station was $29 to $33. Land values around Penn Station were depressed. But the Pennsylvania Railroad could not emulate what the New York Central had done.

In the first place, the Pennsylvania was constrained by high land costs at the time of terminal construction. The New York Central had acquired its land in the mid-nineteenth century, when Manhattan north of 42nd Street was rural and real estate prices were low. The Pennsylvania Railroad was a latecomer. Land in midtown Manhattan was much more expensive in 1902; the Pennsylvania Railroad bought only what was needed for the station, leaving minimal surplus land to develop. The *Wall Street Journal* pinpointed the problem. "Instead of starting its terminal on land costing a minor fraction of its current value, Pennsylvania not only paid modern prices, but gave up a premium created by its desire for and need of other people's property."[112]

Yet money was not an absolute limitation. The Pennsylvania Railroad was a rich corporation; it spent millions every year on railroad improvements and paid an annual dividend to stockholders. The *Wall Street Journal* acknowledged the enormous wealth of the company in 1912: "More than $250,000,000 has poured into the system during the last ten or eleven years and only a very small part of it has been capitalized."[113] The Pennsylvania Railroad was hampered by its own reluctance to enter the business of real estate development. Rea did not lack for good ideas. He wanted to develop the railroad's private street from 33rd to 34th Streets with two large hotels or rows of upscale shops. He also had the idea of buying the entire block south of 31st Street to develop apartment buildings, possibly for the use of railroad employees; the station's power plant on 31st Street would supply the power needs of the apartment buildings.[114] But when developers did not materialize, the railroad retreated. It was unwilling to furnish the capital for new buildings, extend credit, or make ground leases. No development was initiated on 31st or 33rd Streets. The extension to 34th Street was left unimproved; the Greyhound bus terminal was installed for a time. That land as well as the property on Seventh Avenue between 31st and 32nd Streets was sold over time.

Not only was the railroad reluctant to finance development. It did not recognize its potential role in shaping the neighborhood surrounding the station. In 1911 Rea received a smart planning recommendation. It noted that the area around Penn Station lacked office space, especially relative to Grand Central Terminal. Unless office buildings were erected around Penn Station, Grand Central would become the great uptown office center, and suburbanites would choose to live along the New York Central lines. "The right kind of an office building so close to the Pennsylvania Terminal would help not only their suburban business but through traffic as well, as it would surely result in many Western concerns who require offices in New York locating there, who otherwise would locate near the New York Central."[115] Construct prime office space, the report recommended, and other developers will be encouraged to do so. But no one at the Pennsylvania Railroad thought in these long-range planning terms.

In late 1912, the railroad's development plans were in shambles. Its last hope was to build a hotel on Seventh Avenue, and it was more inclined to do so after the Seventh

Avenue subway line won final approval in 1913. The railroad incorporated the Pennsylvania Terminal Real Estate Company to act as its development arm, its first task being to review a dozen hotel proposals for the site between 32nd and 33rd Streets on Seventh Avenue.[116] Rea gave all prospective developers the same advice he offered the representative of the Plaza Hotel: "In developing a plan of building for our property on Seventh Avenue between 32nd and 33rd Streets your Architects must bear in mind its relation to our handsome station on the opposite side of the Street, and that before we would consider a sale or a lease of our property, we would desire to know the character of the structure and whether it was designed in keeping with out station building."[117] In 1916 the Pennsylvania Railroad advanced the sum of about $9.5 million to build the Hotel Pennsylvania, which was designed by William Symmes Richardson of McKim, Mead & White. By an agreement in April 1916, the railroad leased the hotel to a Milwaukee-based operator named Franklin J. Machette who, a few months later, transferred the lease to the Hotel Statler. Originally planned with 1,000 rooms, the hotel opened in January 1919 with 2,200 rooms — the largest hotel in the world (until 1927).[118] Size mattered because the Pennsylvania Railroad's intention was to have its hotel surpass Grand Central's Hotel Biltmore and rank as the largest, most comfortable, and most affordable business hotel in the city.[119]

1.79. Hotel Pennsylvania.

In terms of interior planning, the Hotel Pennsylvania looked to its Grand Central rival, but its facade paid homage to Penn Station. The Hotel Pennsylvania achieved the goal of architectural harmony that Rea had steadfastly supported (Fig. 1.79). The exterior of Indiana limestone reached a height of 62 feet, corresponding to the height of Penn Station. A portico of stone columns echoed the columns of the station as did string courses and other architectural trim. Arguably the single most important feature of the Hotel Pennsylvania was not the architectural treatment of the facade, however, but the pedestrian passageway under 33rd Street that linked the hotel with Penn Station, the subway, and Gimbel's.[120] By the time the Seventh Avenue subway arrived in 1918, the Pennsylvania Railroad had largely retreated behind its granite walls. The Hotel Pennsylvania was its only development in the station area.

Pennsylvania Station functioned as an important transportation node, but it failed to shape a district. The railroad's development efforts were hampered by several factors: high land values when the station site was acquired which limited its acquisition of surplus land; the location of its tracks, which lacked commercial appeal for air-rights development; subway politics which delayed construction of the Seventh and Eighth Avenues lines, which were essential circulation arteries for the station; and an aesthetic vision focused on architectural harmony and unified ensembles which was at odds with the characteristic cacophony of Manhattan's streetscapes and the nature of the real estate market.

The Pennsylvania Railroad was considered the finest railroad in America. "Its rails and rolling stock, its ballast and bridges, its stations and service are regarded as embodying a state of perfection to equal which should be the highest ambition of every railroad company in the country." [121] That was the judgment of a British railroad expert in 1893, and the New York extension, among other initiatives during the following decades, made it an even finer railroad. The most fundamental limitation on the railroad's development efforts was the mission of the Pennsylvania Railroad itself. The Pennsylvania did not see itself in the business of real estate development. Its business was the railroad.

COMMUTERS

Today Penn Station is used mostly by commuters, but it was not planned that way, and for good reason. Commuter lines were handled largely by other facilities. The Pennsylvania Railroad directed its New Jersey–based commuter traffic through the tunnels of the Hudson and Manhattan Railroad to the Hudson Terminal Buildings in downtown Manhattan. An agreement reached between the companies in 1906 gave the Pennsylvania's passengers the option of disembarking at Newark and boarding the H & M's rapid transit trains. Unlike the Pennsylvania, the Long Island Railroad was a commuter line, but it handled the bulk of its suburban traffic at Flatbush Avenue in Brooklyn, which was directly connected with the subway system. The facilities of Penn Station, from track layout and platform width to waiting rooms and restaurants, were planned for long-distance trains and their passengers.

Since the operating assumption was that commuter traffic would play a secondary role, the Long Island Railroad did not get much space in Penn Station. Of the twenty-one tracks, sixteen were for the Pennsylvania's trains, five were for the LIRR. Within this framework, an effort was made to accommodate the LIRR's special needs. Their tracks were located on the north side of the station so that passengers would have easier access to the subways when they eventually opened. The LIRR had its own entrances, ticket offices, and waiting rooms, although waiting was more likely to be done on the platform since the LIRR trains operated on a shuttle basis. At a late stage in the design, the track layout was even modified to widen the shuttle platforms, a change that required moving the north wall of the station closer to 33rd Street. As a result, the driveways were not perfectly symmetric; the 33rd Street driveway was three feet wider.

The Pennsylvania Railroad was wrong about its passenger traffic. It correctly predicted that the number of passengers using Penn Station would increase rapidly. In 1911, the first full year of operation, just under 10 million passengers used the station. In 1920, the number reached 36.5 million. Over the 1920s, there was a 73 percent increase in traffic, bringing the annual number of people in 1929 to 65.6 million. Passenger traffic at Penn Station surpassed that of Grand Central Station in 1919; after that, Grand Central never caught up. The Pennsylvania did not, however, anticipate the dominant role of suburban traffic. The Long Island Railroad accounted for nearly two-thirds of the volume at Penn Station.[122]

Although Penn Station had the capacity to handle half a million travelers daily—a number rarely if ever reached—the growth trends were a problem because the station, from track layout to support spaces, was not designed to serve commuter traffic. The large majority of users were confined to cramped quarters. They moved underground, from commuter shuttles to subways and streets, without cause to enter McKim's uplifting vaulted spaces. Millions of people were using Penn Station, but not as McKim had intended and, more urgently, not as the Pennsylvania Railroad projected on their balance sheets.

REDEVELOPMENT OPTIONS

After World War II, the Pennsylvania Railroad ran into trouble.

One problem was the high cost of operations. In 1951, the Pennsylvania Railroad had to spend 85.5 percent of its operating revenues to pay operating expenses, down from 90.7 percent in 1946. These high numbers meant that the company had inadequate funds to maintain and upgrade equipment, cover other capital expenditures, and return a profit to stockholders. The operating ratio of the Long Island Railroad, a wholly owned subsidiary of the Pennsylvania, was 95 percent, one of the worst ratios in the industry. By contrast, a profitable railroad like the Norfolk & Western had an operating ratio of 67 percent. The Pennsylvania's annual report in 1951 acknowledged the stark reality: "This ratio does not produce a margin sufficient to meet interest, rents, taxes, and other requirements to afford a satisfactory return to the stockholders and provide sufficient funds for reinvestment to continue financial stability."[123]

Another problem was the sharp decline in passenger ridership. In 1939 railroads handled 65 percent of intercity passenger traffic. By 1960 that share fell to 27 percent.[124] The change resulted from the rise of automobile and airplane travel, two rival forms of transportation that the federal government promoted. The government invested hundreds of millions of tax dollars in construction of an interstate highway system. In 1958 alone, government expenditures on highways totaled $10.3 billion. Also in 1958 the federal government allocated $431 million to support the airlines and construction of airports. By contrast, the railroads did not draw public subsidies; they had to manage, like other private businesses, with their own resources. In 1958, the railroad industry spent approximately $1.2 billion on maintenance and construction, and it paid the government $180 million in taxes.[125] But unlike private businesses, the railroads did not have a free hand in making basic business decisions; the Interstate Commerce Commission tightly regulated the industry. The ICC set the passenger rate structure of the railroads as well as their levels of service, compelling companies like the Pennsy to run passenger lines at a deficit. In short, during the 1950s, the government hampered the railroad industry while pouring millions of dollars into competing forms of transportation. Throughout the 1950s and 1960s, the railroads complained, with good reason, that they were not competing on a level playing field. The fate of Pennsylvania Station should be seen in relation to the broader forces that ultimately destroyed not just a landmark building but also the business of passenger train travel.

Ironically, the Pennsylvania Railroad was a victim of its own success. Due in part to Cassatt's acquisition of the Long Island Railroad, the Pennsylvania was the largest passenger railroad in the country. Twenty percent of its rail revenues came from passenger business, a much higher figure than across the industry where, on average, only 13 percent of revenues came from passenger as opposed to freight trains. In the postwar years, the Pennsylvania's relatively high share of passenger business spelled financial disaster. Freight sustained the industry during the 1950s. Railroads are most efficient in moving large quantities of low-value commodities over great distances. Thus a freight railroad like the Norfolk & Western, which primarily transported coal, or a western company like the Union Pacific, which had an average freight haul of 600 miles, compared to 244 miles for the Pennsylvania, continued to make money.[126] The Pennsylvania's freight business also remained profitable, but its passenger business was a major drain. In 1957 the company lost $57 million on its passenger operations.[127] While the passenger train business faced a national decline, the Pennsylvania was more severely affected, in part because of its supremacy in this area, in part because of regional factors. The number of long-distance travelers dwindled, but the demand for rush-hour service into the populous, mainline cities of New York, Philadelphia, and Washington continued. The company had to operate a fleet of well-maintained trains sufficient to meet peak demand but only for a few hours, leaving equipment and labor idle most of the day. Moreover, the Pennsylvania faced high terminal costs, with large train yards on expensive real estate in inner cities.

These pressures resulted in ever increasing passenger deficits that the Pennsylvania, the nation's leading passenger line, could not avoid. The only way the Pennsylvania survived from the 1950s on, explained Stuart Saunders, who served as president during the company's final years, was by tapping sources of outside income to compensate for passenger deficits and by selling off assets at a rate of about $50 million a year.[128] Forced to cannibalize its business to stay alive, the railroad company targeted Penn Station.

The redevelopment of the Penn Station site, which occupied nine valuable acres in midtown Manhattan, was part of the company's efforts to reduce high terminal expenses and to maximize the value of its assets. The company's goal was to erase the station's operating deficit and to produce the maximum income for the railroad. "Under present day conditions, the Pennsylvania Station property is not being used to best advantage and in many respects is an economic waste . . . ," a company official explained in a private memorandum in 1950. "Any plausible scheme for development is worthy of further consideration provided the price to us is right."[129]

The first public signal of the Pennsylvania's intentions came in 1950 when the City Planning Commission approved a six-story, 800-car garage above the south courtyard of the station.[130] The railroad failed to see the absurdity of accommodating drivers at an inner-city transportation hub, but the garage idea disappeared as the railroad searched for a better deal. In 1952 the company received an offer from H. B. Cantor, president of the Hotel Governor Clinton, located on Seventh Avenue a block south of the station. Cantor proposed a mixed-use development, including an amphitheater, office building, hotel, garage, and stores. He offered $29.5 million for the entirety of Pennsylvania Station, including the space underground, with a leaseback arrangement whereby the railroad would pay an annual rent of $2 million for office space and the station facilities. Cantor's price was too low; the annual lease obligation of $2 million would have exceeded the savings of $1.6 million in annual operating expenses. In evaluating Cantor's proposal, company officials identified the basic terms of a deal they could accept. First, those portions of Penn Station above street level would be demolished, leaving the underground area more or less intact. Second, the railroad would retain ownership of the station. Third, the air rights would be sold for $50 million. The decision to destroy Penn Station was essentially made in 1952 for a price of $50 million—a one-time cash infusion that probably would not even cover the company's passenger deficits for a year. From the railroad's perspective, Penn Station was a huge and unjustifiable overhead expense. The accountants had no way of factoring in their balance sheets the historical and urban value of the station. One official captured the prevailing attitude: "I feel that the prospect of disposing of Pennsylvania Station, New York, on a proper basis is definitely worthy of consideration.

We certainly have no feeling for the monumental value of Pennsylvania Station as compared to an annual return, before taxes, of over $1,000,000 [from a prospective development]."[131]

Another suitor appeared in early 1953 when Webb & Knapp, the real estate firm headed by William Zeckendorf, began discussions with the Pennsylvania Railroad about the totality of its air rights. In September 1953, Zeckendorf signed an option to buy the air rights above the tracks west of Ninth Avenue for $4 million; his plan was to build a commercial structure topped by a heliport.[132] A year later, in November 1954, Zeckendorf signed an option for the air rights above the station for the purpose of building a $100 million international merchandise mart, dubbed the Palace of Progress. Zeckendorf's project was grandiose. "If carried out," the *New York Times* reported in a front-page story, "the project would provide a skyscraper 500 feet high, with nearly 7,000,000 square feet of floor space, that would be the world's largest and costliest building—a permanent world's fair, wholesaling center and buyers' headquarters."[133] A 1950s vision of high-tech, the Palace of Progress was conceived to exploit the possibilities of television merchandising: every floor would be equipped with lighting, acoustics, and cable to serve as a set for television or closed-circuit broadcasts, enabling tenants "to use television to achieve point of sales contact."[134] Zeckendorf installed the celebrity showman Billy Rose as president of the subsidiary company to market the building and lobbied the Secretary of Commerce to exempt foreign goods displayed at the "palace" from U.S. import tariffs. The Pennsylvania Railroad approved the air-rights sale for $30 million, well below its asking price of $50 million. Moreover, the railroad agreed to dedicate $13 million to reconstruction of an entirely underground station. A financial analysis of Zeckendorf's offer showed that annual maintenance, utilities, and taxes on the station amounted to $3,285,600. The railroad retained costs below sidewalk level estimated at $2,113,600. Thus the resulting savings in operating costs was only $1,172,000.[135] A drop in the bucket considering the financial plight of the railroad.

The news of Zeckendorf's scheme stirred excitement and some skepticism, but not a word of protest. The *New York Times* approved the railroad's decision "to make more profitable use of valuable real estate holdings" and commended Zeckendorf's ambitious project. "New York, which sees in the new plans an encouraging confirmation of confidence in the city's prosperous future, will await with eagerness and interest the full shape of things to come in the way of blueprints."[136] Whatever preservation-oriented concerns lurked in the hearts of New Yorkers did not register on the public screen. It is striking that the many articles on the Palace of Progress in New York's leading newspapers, the *New York Times* and the *Herald Tribune,* did not once use the word "demolition" to describe the fate of McKim's station. Here is a typical description of the project from the

New York Times: "The plans for Pennsylvania Station, if consummated, would call for the complete modernization of the passenger station—busiest in the nation—below street level and the erection of an entirely new building . . . above street level."[137] Reporters described the changes in wholly positive terms and failed to make explicit the necessary pre-condition—removal of a monument. Big as the station was, it was overlooked because, at least in public discourse, no value was attached to the architectural quality of the city.

One person saw it as it was: Lawrence Grant White, son of Stanford White and head of McKim, Mead & White. After learning of Zeckendorf's intention to demolish Pennsylvania Station, White met with the developer. "I lunched yesterday with William Zeckendorf, who said that he was negotiating with the P.R.R. [Pennsylvania Railroad] for the Pennsylvania Station in New York, with the avowed purpose of tearing it down and erecting a 30 story building upon the site. I had already told him at a previous dinner that I deplored tearing down such an important building, but afraid neither I nor my firm could do anything to stop it; and that if it was to be torn down we would like, as architects for the P.R.R., to have some professional connection with the building that was to be erected. . . . After an excellent lunch in his fabulous setting, he promised to keep us in mind."[138] White's words poignantly reflect the prevailing mindset—protest was futile, demolition appeared inevitable, and profitable redevelopment was a common goal.

Zeckendorf's option expired in July 1956. He attempted to renew it on revised terms, lowering his purchase price from $30 million to $10 million, an offer which James Symes, president of the Pennsylvania Railroad, promptly rejected. "The venture is unattractive from an economic standpoint. Additionally, we believe it better at this time to retain con-

1.80. Project to replace the east end of Pennsylvania Station along Seventh Avenue with a parking lot, 1960.

1.81 Project to replace the east
end of Pennsylvania Station
along Seventh Avenue with
two high-rise buildings, 1960.

trol of the entire Station property—so that we will be in position to adequately protect
the needs of railroad patrons using the facility."[139] Though invoking the Pennsylvania's
traditional values—the priority accorded to railroad needs—Symes was in fact fully committed to a new financial strategy of diversifying the company's investments in non-railroad holdings and was holding out for a more lucrative development offer.

After the collapse of Zeckendorf's highly publicized project, no other deals were forth-
coming. In 1959 the railroad launched a study of the structural changes and station alterations involved in an air-rights development. While the study was under way, the possibility of demolishing all or part of the station and building high-rise towers was raised;
even a temporary parking lot at street level was favored over preserving the station (Figs
1.80 and 1.81). The Pennsylvania Railroad was operating the station at an annual loss of $1.5
million. Removing the aboveground portions of the station would have reduced the railroad's operating costs by only $300,000, but Symes believed an empty site would motivate
developers to step forward.[140] The internal study, issued in March 1960, outlined two possible redevelopment schemes: one consisting of four 20-story towers, the other combining a 50-story tower with a quadrangle of low-rise buildings.[141]

On the occasion of the station's half-centennial on September 10, 1960, the *New York
Times* published an appreciation—a dramatic reversal of the paper's dismissive views during the 1950s: "For a fifty-year old masterpiece of civic pride and cosmopolitan symbolism,
the Pennsylvania Station is still impressive."[142] Not to its owners. The Pennsylvania
Railroad did not feel pride; it was coming undone by operating losses. For only the second
time in its 116-year history the company reported a deficit in 1960 (the first time was in 1946).
The passenger business reported a net operating loss of $30,877,000, but income from oth-
er sources reduced the company's total deficit to $7.8 million.[143] The company needed addi-
tional and more profitable outside investments to sustain the passenger business.

Around 1960, David Bevan, vice-president for finance, charted a new strategy of diversification involving the railroad's real estate holdings. Don't sell the company's valuable

acreage in cities like New York, Philadelphia, and Chicago, he argued. The railroad stands to make more money by leasing the air rights and taking an equity position in the new developments, thereby providing the company with an income stream from non-railroad activities. The first such project credited to Bevan was in the company's hometown of Philadelphia, on the site of the old Broad Street Station, which the railroad had demolished in 1952. Unwilling to take on any further obligations, President Symes was prepared to sell the 17-acre site to a developer for $10 million, but when that deal collapsed, Bevan was given a shot. The deal he structured in 1960 gave the Pennsylvania Railroad equity in the Penn Center, a complex of office buildings, apartments, and hotels that indeed generated money for the railroad. In 1963 the company received $25 million for air rights over trackage and $550,000 in rentals.[144] This prototype was emulated even more successfully in New York City.

The owners of Madison Square Garden wanted to build a new sports arena. The investment house of Graham-Paige headed by Irving Mitchell Felt had bought the Garden, then located at Eighth Avenue between 49th and 50th Streets, in January 1959, and began searching for a new site in November 1960. The Pennsylvania Railroad approached Felt and suggested Penn Station. Although the railroad had recently decided to erect a 40-story tower, it was ready to scrap that plan in favor of more intensive development and a richer deal.[145] The parties reached an agreement in July 1961; the final contract was dated October 18, 1963. Rather than sell the air rights, the Pennsylvania Railroad gave the Madison Square Garden Center a long-term lease (with renewal rights, it came to 99 years). The *Wall Street Journal* reported that the railroad would receive a minimum of $1.5 million in rental income a year. In fact, the lease provided for smaller sums, stepping up from $400,000 for the first 16 months to $1 million annually beginning in 1965.[146] The rental income would offset but not extinguish the operating losses at Penn Station, which were put at $2.5 million in 1961.[147] But the railroad derived another source of income by virtue of its 25 percent ownership of the Madison Square Garden Center Corporation, which was formed to undertake the new development. Graham-Paige owned a 75 percent interest and agreed to provide all the equity. While the Pennsylvania Railroad did not have to put up any cash, it agreed to spend $20 million to demolish McKim's building, remodel the station, and build the slab foundation for Madison Square Garden. The railroad's direct investment in Madison Square Garden Center as well as its 55 percent interest in the corporation's other investments opened a valuable revenue stream.[148]

The centerpiece of the development was, of course, Madison Square Garden, an arena seating 22,000 people. As Bevan had correctly foreseen, real estate investments such as Madison Square Garden were not necessarily incompatible with railroad activities. Ever since the first ballparks were built at the end of tramlines in the late nineteenth century, the combination of transit station and sports stadium was a winning formula. Trains and subways at Penn Station could easily handle the crowds attending games at Madison Square Garden, while the pedestrian traffic during off-hours was good for the railroads. The original project also included a 4,000-seat arena eventually named the Felt Forum (after Irving Mitchell Felt, the controlling shareholder), a bowling center, and a 12-story garage for 3,000 cars, a counterproductive element that was subsequently dropped. Plans for towers situated along the Seventh Avenue frontage evolved over time. At first, they called for a 34-story office tower and a 28-story hotel with 750 rooms, then twin office buildings. When the two main tenants pulled out in May 1963, the developers decided to build the sports facilities first and to scale back the office buildings. Eventually one tower was built, called One Penn Plaza.[149]

Penn Center, Philadelphia; Madison Square Garden, New York — and later, Gateway Center in Chicago — while these real estate projects were integral to the railroad's program of diversification, they were not critical elements of the Pennsylvania's long-term survival strategy. The strategy plotted by James Symes was to merge the Pennsylvania Railroad with its chief rival, the New York Central. Among the problems of the railroad industry was excess capacity — too many trains carrying too few passengers. Symes argued that consolidation and reduction of the number of railroads was the only way for the industry to avoid a wave of bankruptcies, which, he ominously predicted, would lead to nationalization of the railways. Symes believed that the forty-odd eastern railroads should merge into two or three systems, one of them headed by the Pennsylvania Railroad.[150] With that goal in mind, Symes opened merger discussions with New York Central on November 1, 1957. After an interruption in 1960 while the companies explored other merger possibilities, talks resumed in October 1961. Both boards approved the merger on January 12, 1962, whereupon the Interstate Commerce Commission began an extended review. The companies argued that the merger would harvest savings by enabling them to use the most efficient routes, reduce operating expenses, and sell excess facilities. The railroads announced that the estimated annual savings would amount to $81 million.[151]

The merger and the redevelopment of Penn Station were launched at virtually the same time. The former was hailed as a long-term structural solution, which served to underscore the expedient and short-term nature of the plans for the station.

The Interstate Commerce Commission approved the merger of the Pennsylvania Railroad and the New York Central in 1966, although court challenges delayed the creation of the Penn Central until February 1, 1968. The merger was a spectacular failure. After barely two years (871 days), Penn Central declared bankruptcy on June 21, 1970 — the largest corporate bankruptcy up to that time. Although various factors came into play, the chief explanation for Penn Central's collapse was "the unprecedented breakdown of operations in the merged company"; the companies never really merged.[152] As for the projected annual savings of $81 million, business historians have found that careful financial analysis did not undergird the estimate; it was more or less fictitious. As James Symes had predicted, bankruptcy led to nationalization of the railroads. Long-distance passenger train service was taken over by Amtrak, a quasi-public entity chartered by Congress on May 1, 1971. The Long Island Railroad was also rescued by governmental intervention. In 1965 the State of New York took control of the bankrupt commuter line, which was then operated by the Metropolitan Commuter Transportation Authority, a state agency. The Pennsylvania Railroad received $65 million in cash plus tax relief and other benefits amounting to $120 million.

DEMOLITION

The demolition of Penn Station was headline news from 1961 until the last stone was removed in 1966. Not that the demolition of Penn Station came as a surprise: "The railroad has been trying for ten years to get someone to help it rid itself of what had become a white elephant," a reporter correctly pointed out.[153] But the attitude of the press and the public had evolved quickly since 1955, when the prospect of Zeckendorf's palace elicited only praise and wonderment. New York City was riding a wave of commercial development; entire blocks of historic townhouses were swept away by mediocre new structures. Most significantly, in 1960 the *New York Times* began to champion the cause of historic preservation; it ran frequent editorials on the subject, hired Ada Louise Huxtable to write on architectural topics, and gave prominent and stirring coverage to the demolition of Penn Station as well as other historic buildings.

An advertisement in the *New York Times* on August 3, 1962, invited New Yorkers to attend a protest rally at Penn Station. The organizers, Action Group for Better Architecture in New York (AGBANY), conceded that it was too late to save the station; their real purpose was broader: "Penn Station, one of our finest structures . . . is about to be demolished—just as the Ritz, the Murray Hill and the Marguery were destroyed to make more room for still more profit-making square footage. It may be too late to save Penn Station; next month the wreckers will move in for the kill. But it is not yet too late to save New York. We, the undersigned—architects, artists, architectural historians, and citizens of New York—serve notice upon the present and future would-be vandals that we will fight them every step of the way. New York's architecture is a major part of our heritage. We intend to see it preserved."[154]

It is significant that the signatories of the statement were nearly all avowed modernists: Philip Johnson, Romaldo Giurgola, J. J. P. Oud, Paul Rudolph, Aline Saarinen, Hugh

Stubbins, Robert Venturi, and Thomas Creighton, editor of *Progressive Architecture*, to name a few. In another sign of change, the cause of modernism realigned itself with historic architecture. Turnout at the rally was small, only 150 to 200 marchers, but their cultural prominence amplified the effect. The rally garnered front-page coverage in the *New York Times* as well as editorial praise: "What they were protesting at the moment was the increasing, irreplaceable loss of New York's architectural past through irresponsible, speculative building. . . . With minimum controls New York's builders are well on their way to turning the city into a bottomless—and topless—morass of mediocrity."[155]

Talk of architecture made no sense to the Pennsylvania Railroad. A. J. Greenough, president of the company, responded to AGBANY's protest in a letter to the editor of the *New York Times*. "Does it make any sense to attempt to preserve a building merely as a 'monument' when it no longer serves the utilitarian needs for which it was erected?" he asked. "It was built by private enterprise by the way, and not primarily as a monument at all but as a railroad station."[156] Never mind Greenough's failure to understand that the station was conceived precisely as a civic monument; a bigger obstacle was his blindness to the extraordinary status the building had achieved. Though privately owned and operated, Pennsylvania Station had been thoroughly absorbed into city life. It was regarded not as private property but as a civic structure and a public resource. To New Yorkers, Penn Station was part of the public sphere, but the railroad was responsible to its shareholders. "Who subsidizes the Pennsylvania Railroad?" asked Irving Mitchell Felt.[157] The dilemma was clearly formulated by Norval White, the founder of AGBANY and assistant professor of urban design at Cooper Union. "The Pennsylvania Railroad should not be made to suffer economically for the current bad economics of the structure. But similarly, the citizenry of our city should not be made to suffer from the economic exploitation of an important monument and symbol, an important gateway to the nation."[158]

A solution required the intervention of a public authority. White made an interesting proposal, in fact the only alternative that was offered. He suggested a takeover by the Port of New York Authority (now known as Port Authority of New York and New Jersey), which operated a variety of gateways to the city—the George Washington Bridge, the area airports (Newark, La Guardia, and Idlewild, now J.F.K.), the shipping ports, as well as truck and bus terminals.[159] Since the 1930s, the Port Authority had steadfastly refused any involvement with passenger rail service because, it argued, a deficit operation would hinder the Authority's ability to finance its projects. Only under immense political pressure did the Port Authority agree in 1960 to take over the Hudson and Manhattan commuter railroad (thereafter renamed the Port Authority Trans-Hudson, or PATH Corporation).[160] The Authority was not about to subsidize the Pennsylvania Railroad. Nor was any governmental body.

Rallies could not save the station. Citizen protests had sometimes succeeded in the past. When plans to demolish Carnegie Hall were announced in 1959, a rescue committee headed by violinist Isaac Stern managed to save the hall; in 1965 the Percy Pyne Mansion was rescued when the Marquesa de Cuevas bought the house and donated it to what became the Americas Society. Penn Station was too big to be saved by philanthropic gestures, and protests had begun long after the station's fate was sealed. The fundamental problem was that New York City had no mechanisms in place to protect landmarks and provide remedies. There were no laws to prevent demolition or to designate historic landmarks. In order to build an arena with more than 2,500 seats, Madison Square Garden had only to obtain a zoning variance from the City Planning Commission. In early 1963 the commission granted the variance.[161]

Demolition began on October 28, 1963, with the ceremonial removal of a nearly three-ton eagle from the 33rd Street entrance. The main clock was set at 10:53 to mark the short lifespan of the building: it had opened in 1910 and stood for only 53 years. It took three years to demolish the structure and simultaneously build Madison Square Garden. Throughout construction, the train station remained operational; traffic of nearly 600 trains and 200,000 passengers continued to use the station daily.[162]

1.82. Granite blocks from Pennsylvania Station in the Seacaucus Meadows, N.J., April 1965.

An editorial in the *New York Daily News* on October 30, 1963, accepted the demolition of Penn Station as the necessary price of progress: "The fact is that no busy location in Manhattan can indefinitely support a two-story building, however reminiscent of ancient Rome. Taxes are too high. The new structure . . . may not be a beauty . . . but at least it will be convenient." The *New York Times* sounded a tragic note: "A rich and powerful city, noted for its resources of brains, imagination and money, could not rise to the occasion. The final indictment is of the values of our society."[163]

Work proceeded in three overlapping stages. First, a low ceiling was inserted in McKim's train concourse, decapitating the vaulted region and lowering the height of the concourse from 90 to 24 feet. In that radically truncated space, passengers continued to make use of the original concourse floor and train platforms. In the second stage, the aboveground parts of the station were dismantled—first the lateral facades and driveways, next the waiting hall, then the concourse and arcade. The Seventh Avenue facade was preserved until the very end, its massive stones reduced to a shallow screen wall. It came down in 1966–67. The drums of the Doric columns and other blocks of granite, including some and perhaps all of the sculpted figures, were trucked to the Secaucus Meadowlands, where they lay exposed for several years (Figure 1.82). Individuals salvaged some statues and stone elements. Three of the four pairs of statues of Day and Night have been located. One pair forms the centerpiece of the Eagle Scout Tribute Fountain in Kansas City, Missouri. Another pair stands in Ringwood State Park in northern New Jersey. The Brooklyn Museum owns a Night, and the Con Agg Recycling Corporation owns a Day, which would have been pulverized but for some attentive workers who in 1995 recognized that it was not typical salvage and set it aside. The whereabouts of the last two statues are unknown; presumably they were destroyed. Other pieces of Penn Station—eagles, column drums, balusters, clocks, and lamps—were rescued from the Meadowlands by various individuals and lie scattered across the metropolitan region.[164] Other blocks were used as fill in swampy sections or crushed to powder by stone recycling companies. In the final stage of the building process, Madison Square Garden was erected on the cleared site, the lowered ceiling of the concourse serving as the floor of the sports arena. Designed by Charles Luckman, the Garden was completed a year after the last stone was removed and officially opened on February 11, 1968.

Many photographers, both amateurs and professionals, including Peter Moore, Mark Freeman, Aaron Rose, Ron Ziel, and Norman McGrath, were moved by a personal sense of loss to document the demolition.[165] Their photographs, including those by Norman McGrath that are featured in this book, were not exhibited at the time and have remained almost entirely unseen. One amateur photographer eloquently explained his "need to somehow mitigate the shock and ensuing agony . . . upon learning of the architectural holocaust about to be committed."[166] But the photographic work also reveals a fascination with the striking structural forms that appeared as the station was torn down. In some of McGrath's photographs, the station appears as a ruin, its grand spaces rendered strangely silent. In other pictures, cranes and drills besiege the building and strip the steel frame bare. Without the waiting hall to join them, the arcade and concourse look like amputated parts. Still other pictures convey the complex choreography of the construction process. Lilliputian passengers mill on the train concourse as the giant red girders of Madison Square Garden, weighing twenty-three and thirty tons, hover overhead and sever McKim's vaults.

LANDMARKS

The demolition of Pennsylvania Station did not launch the historic preservation movement in New York City. For nearly a decade, the Municipal Art Society, the New York Community Trust, and other civic and professional groups had quietly but persistently been promoting an awareness of historic preservation in a city famously indifferent to the past.[167] Unlike Charleston, New Orleans, or Boston, cities with traditions of preservation going back to the early decades of the century, New York took no notice of its great architectural legacy. Activists had to begin by taking stock of the city's historic buildings. In 1957 the Municipal Art Society published the first list of buildings in New York City worthy of preservation. Three hundred buildings were on the list—fewer than expected because the authors found that "almost a third of the buildings they had planned to include had already been torn down."[168] A growing campaign to preserve historic New York was already under way in 1961 when the Pennsylvania Railroad announced the fate of its station, but that event moved the cause from a circle of cognoscenti into the public eye; it put historic preservation on the front page and into political debate. The loss of Penn Station stirred the conscience of the city.

In July 1961, only days before the railroad's announcement, Mayor Robert Wagner formed a Committee for the Preservation of Structures of Historic and Aesthetic Importance to develop a program to preserve historic buildings. In April 1962, in accordance with the committee's recommendation, Wagner appointed a Landmarks Preservation Commission for the purpose of "protecting structures and areas of historic or esthetic importance." Wagner's action responded to the outcry about Penn Station, but as Geoffrey Platt, chairman of the newly formed Landmarks Preservation Commission, indicated in one of his first public statements, the commission had come into being too late to save the terminal.[169] As constituted in 1962, the Landmarks Preservation Commission was powerless; it could decide which structures were worth saving, but it had no legislative authority to save them. The group's primary responsibility was to develop a detailed legislative program, a task completed on May 7, 1964, when a draft bill was forwarded to the mayor. According to the recollections of two key players — Platt and his successor, Harmon Goldstone — the historic preservation movement found a guardian angel in the unlikely form of James Felt, chairman of the City Planning Commission. Felt brought the issue to the mayor, convinced him to take the initial steps, guided the preservation activists through the political process, and actively participated in drafting the bill.[170] We can only wonder about the hidden sibling drama that led James Felt to champion historic preservation at the very moment that his brother, Irving Mitchell Felt, was tearing down Penn Station.

Meanwhile the pace of destruction seemed to quicken. A row of cast-iron buildings on Worth Street were razed in 1962. The demolitions of the Percy Pyne Mansion on Park Avenue and of the Brokaw houses on Fifth Avenue and 79th Street were announced in 1964.[171] Politicians in all parties, Republican, Democratic, and Liberal, joined the rising crusade for historic preservation and attacked the inaction of Mayor Wagner, who comforted the worried real estate community by ignoring the bill sitting for months on his desk. The *New York Times* offered a scorching editorial on December 3, 1964: "Without time to find ways and means of saving a building, without the consideration of city purchase, and without adequate owner compensation for any possible losses — all of which are provided in this bill — the future is predictably and dismally sure. Not only the city's landmarks, but to a large extent its character and architectural quality are doomed. The private pillage of the public patrimony has long since ceased to be justifiable; it is now a matter of serious public concern. New York has had enough of unrestricted destruction."[172]

In response to mounting pressure, Wagner forwarded the bill to the city council, where it sailed through, easily passing on April 6, 1965.[173] The law creating the Landmarks Preservation Commission was signed on April 19, 1965. In addition to designation powers, the commission was given significant authority to intervene and protect endangered landmarks. The law provided for a period of time during which the commission could craft a rescue plan. The plan had to assure the owner of a reasonably profitable return from his property. Moreover, the law permitted the city to grant property tax remissions or exemptions. If the commission failed to negotiate a preservation plan with the landmark owner, the city had the right to purchase the landmark or take it over through condemnation.

To address concerns of the real estate community, the city council revised some elements of the original bill, but realtors did not mount a forceful attack on the historic preservation legislation. Some observers have attributed the relative quiescence of developers to a conviction that the law was unconstitutional and the Supreme Court would ultimately throw it out. The case that tested the constitutionality of historic preservation reprised several elements of Penn Station's story. The Penn Central, the company resulting from the merger of the Pennsylvania Railroad and the New York Central, decided to demolish Grand Central Terminal and sell the air rights. In 1969 the Landmarks Preservation Commission, which had designated the station as a landmark in 1967, blocked Penn Central's plan to build a skyscraper, designed by Marcel Breuer, above the station. The main concourse would have been retained, but not the waiting hall along 42nd Street. For a fleeting moment in July 1961, the Pennsylvania Railroad had considered retaining the waiting hall of Penn Station and building special connecting ramps to the Garden. Perhaps the idea was renewed at Grand Central in hopes of appeasing preservationists, but they were now armed with legal powers and remedies.

The case of Penn Central Transportation Co. vs. the City of New York reached the U.S. Supreme Court in 1978. The court held that, contrary to the claim of the Penn Central that it had been subject to a taking without just compensation, no taking had occurred, "since the terminal could still be used and a reasonable return on investment could still be earned." Writing for the majority, Justice William Brennan endorsed the public interest in the quality of the built environment: "Underlying the opinion is the notion that aesthetic values, particularly historic preservation, are important public interests that justify restrictions on private land."[174] Grand Central Terminal was saved and, in its wake, hundreds of other landmarks.

Since its establishment in 1965, the Landmarks Preservation Commission has designated over sixty historic districts and more than one thousand individual buildings in New York City. The challenge of historic preservation has become more complex and now centers on the issue of adaptive reuse: how to respect the historic character of a landmark but equip it to function in the modern world. Once again Pennsylvania Station compels us to assess the limits and possibilities of preservation. The creation of the new train station has required alterations to the landmark Farley Post Office. Purists regard that as a loss, yet the changes have the effect of turning a forbidden citadel over to public use.

As this book goes to press, newspapers report that Madison Square Garden will be demolished.[175] It lacks luxury boxes and is too small. It is no longer economic. A fitting conclusion.

Part 2

A Landmark Dismantled:
A Photographic Essay

Norman McGrath

Certain events stand out in the life of any great city. They take a variety of forms. Some are natural in origin—floods, heat waves, and snowstorms, for example. Others are social, more unpredictable, and at times more difficult to accept: the removal of Pennsylvania Station is clearly in this category.

I was born in London, a city of major railroad stations, exciting places that rivaled cathedrals for sheer size and grandeur. I remember massive, streamlined steam locomotives from before World War II and viewed railroad stations as a permanent component of the urban scene. I came to New York City from Dublin in 1956, a structural engineer by profession, but a serious amateur photographer. In the early 1960s I found myself jobless and felt the timing was right to make a career change. I bought myself a 4 x 5 view camera and set out to teach myself its idiosyncrasies. Two or three months later, I had a call from a former associate who had heard of my intended career switch and wondered if I was "interested in eating in the meantime." The upshot was that I went to work as an engineer for Wayman C. Wing on a part-time basis while I made the transition from one profession to another. My new office was in the Hotel Pennsylvania, right across from Penn Station.

I had a number of good friends who were professional photographers, including Aaron Rose, Francis Keavney (fellow Irishman), and Will Forbes, who ran a darkroom service. Pennsylvania Station became something of an obsession for the four of us. We explored the enormous building in groups, cameras in hand, though I did not see their photographs. Since a condition of the demolition was the continued operation of the station, the building could not be closed. This, of course, greatly added to the already complex task of dismantling so large an edifice. The resulting security of what was simultaneously a construction and demolition site was somewhat haphazard. On our many forays into the disappearing building I do not recall a single instance of being challenged. (In retrospect I suppose I could have tried to obtain official permission for my documentation, but my credentials were thin.) In any event, we frequently photographed on weekends, which did not compromise construction or demolition work and gave us almost complete freedom of movement. Our ability to move about, through, into, around and all over the building was invaluable, though not without hazard.

In the early stages of demolition, much of the terminal was unknown to me. Every visit became an adventure into the past, to spaces that had served some forgotten function, mundane or grand. The parts of Penn Station occupying the eastern and western side, fronting Seventh and Eighth Avenues, housed various offices, some relating to the railroad, others not. Over two thousand railroad employees worked in the building. In all, almost three thousand people made their living there.

While I was photographing the demolition, I attended a series of workshops taught by Alexey Brodovitch, the Russian-born art director of *Harper's Bazaar* from 1934 to 1958 who gave Richard Avedon his first assignment; the classes were held weekly in Avedon's studio, and he sometimes participated. At every session, Brodovitch encouraged personal assignments, stressing the necessity to come up with something exciting and different. Some of the results were quite straightforward, others very elaborate. Presentations were made to the whole class in whatever form the photographer chose. Brodovitch did not disguise his disapproval if he felt it was warranted, but his harsh criticism seemed to provoke ever greater efforts to produce results that would earn his praise.

I chose the demolition of Penn Station as my project. I looked at Penn Station with new eyes and saw things I might otherwise have missed. Working on a daily basis just across the street meant that I could keep a watchful eye on the progress of work and have a reasonable chance of being able to record particularly dramatic events, like the removal of the guardian eagles. I focused on the regular users of the station and recorded their sometime tortuous paths through the compromised facility. The group photographs of people, mostly men, watching the workers dismantle the station piece by piece, reflect the fascination of pedestrians in both the demolition and construction processes being carried out simultaneously.

I tried to relate my photographs of the station to its surroundings, sometimes including the familiar profile of the Empire State Building or the neighboring Post Office, so later viewers could relate photographs to still-standing structures. The roof of the Hotel Pennsylvania afforded an all-encompassing view of the site; I also climbed into the roof structures of the station and stood above the vaults to gain a high vantage point. Often the route was tortuous, and retracing my tracks to a particular location difficult because the station was constantly changing.

During the 1960s all important architectural documentation was done in black and white, and the publications devoted to architecture were entirely black and white. While I had started my documentation in both color and black and white, I felt that color would have an impact on a wider audience. Nevertheless, the importance of quality black and white architectural photographs led me to take a limited number of 4″ x 5″ images of the station with my view camera. Most of my black and white photographs of Penn Station were taken with a Brooks Plaubel Veriwide 100 camera. It was physically not much larger than a 35mm camera but had an unusual format of 2¼″ x 3½″ on 120mm film. The large negative size yielded high quality enlargements. The camera was a rangefinder type designed around Schneider's 47mm f 8.0 lens, which was capable of taking extremely wide-angle views, 100 degrees across the diagonal. The lens, though slow at f 8.0, was extremely sharp; even at maximum aperture with a focal length of 47mm, it had very good depth of sharp focus, with the lens wide open, using its very simple zone focusing scale. The camera had two levels so that distortion could be kept to a minimum with a tripod. The Leica viewfinder made the camera very easy to use. I used Kodak Tri-X for all the black and white work on the station.

Not until the 1970s was the switch to color for architectural photographs brought about by pressure from advertisers and by improvements in reproduction technology. The change from black and white to color happened very fast, and it made finding a high-quality printer for black and white images increasingly difficult. It is no longer possible to duplicate my prints from the 1960s: not only have the printing techniques changed, but also the black and white paper used for the originals is no longer available.

By photographing Penn Station in color and in small format (35 mm), I was much more mobile and could avoid, except in very dark interiors, using a tripod, which would have been difficult to set up in the precarious locations I found myself in. Moreover, color photographs had a more reportage-like character. The main handicap in using a small format camera for architectural subjects in the 1960s, whether in black and white or color, was the lack of lenses with perspective control (PC). I used one of the few PC lenses then available, a moderately wide angle Nikkor 35mm PC lens. A PC lens allows the photographer to adjust the normal optical axis and thereby to extend the composition in a particular direction while maintaining the camera level; in this way the composition of the photograph can be adjusted without tilting and thereby introducing distortion. A truly level camera also minimizes some of the disturbing distortions that can arise when using any very wide-angle optic. A tripod makes leveling easier. With large-format view cameras, all the lenses are adjustable, which make them the first choice of architectural photographers. But I liked the small format and wide-angle views. With careful composition and the use of one-point perspective—that is keeping the axis of the lens perpendicular to the plane of the main subject—I was able to minimize distortion. One of the main penalties for using extreme wide angle lenses is spatial exaggeration; spaces look bigger.

At the time Kodachrome II was the best-quality film available. Kodachrome is a roll format film, available only in 35mm, so it was not an option for the Veriwide or my 4 x 5 view camera. Among color films, it had the finest grain, best resolution and contrast, and most important, was archivally superior. With a speed of 25 ASA, it was twice as fast as the film it had replaced (Kodachrome I with a speed of only 12 ASA), but by today's standards, Kodachrome II was slow. I also used Ektachrome X 64 ASA, which was faster but lacked the punch of Kodachrome and was not as archivally safe, and some Ansco film, which was faster but required special processing and proved not very stable over the long run.

My slides of Penn Station have been stored in several different ways, none, however, in a particularly archival manner. Surprisingly, most have survived well. Although there has been some color shift, only a few are unusable. The Kodachromes remain virtually unscathed by the ravages of time and look as good today as when I took them.

Aaron Rose stored his exposed but undeveloped film in a deep freeze. (Somehow, by not developing the film, he felt he was postponing the inevitable.) Thirty-five years later, I suggested that he see if anything survived on those frozen rolls. Not surprisingly, time had caused considerable fogging, an effect that only seemed to enhance the prints. It was like looking in an old mirror, back into the past. Aaron Rose has since donated his Penn Station prints to the Museum of the City of New York.

The demolition work began slowly, with just a few warning signs here and there and the odd barricade. Some of the contractors' signs suggested ambivalence about what they were doing: "Sorry, but!" The contractors seemed to be probing their target for weak spots to attack, like wolves circling their prey awaiting the right opportunity. Once they decided where to start, the going was rough. The building was solid—at least the exterior walls were. The massive granite columns were designed to last indefinitely. Chipping away at their bases seemed an exercise in futility, but little by little, the persistent gnawing began to make an impact. Despite the noise from jack hammers and acetylene burners and great clouds of dust pierced by cascades of sparks, commuters and long-distance travelers largely ignored the battle, threading their way through the maze of obstructions that seemed to grow daily.

Then came a major surprise. The great waiting room, the main space in the terminal, seemingly as solid as the exterior, turned out to be like a giant stage set. The masonry was only a veneer supported by a metal framework. Each of the massive interior columns was plaster, with a steel section of modest dimensions at its core. The coffered ceiling was easily peeled off, revealing a web of steel supports, not nearly as generous as one might have expected. So much for the impression of solidity. Unlike the unyielding granite facade, the interior virtually crumbled. This portion of the demolition work proceeded speedily, with changes evident almost daily.

I put together one or two slide shows for my Brodovitch classes; they were well received and elicited his praise. I showed my material to various magazines, architectural and otherwise, but it did not provoke much response at the time. Once the fate of the station was sealed, people seemed unconcerned. A few of us mourned, but the majority assumed that old buildings had to be sacrificed in the interest of progress. I put away my demolition archive. A few black and white photographs have been published over the years, but the color photographs are published in this book for the first time.

All that remains of the old station is our ever-dimming recollection of it, and the photographic record.

Norman McGrath at Penn Station, c. 1964. Photograph by Aaron Rose.

opposite

2.1. Train concourse facing the 33rd Street entrance as demolition begins. The steel frame of the new ceiling is beginning to encroach on the right.

2.2. Pedestrian bridge over the 33rd Street driveway. Demolition began with removal of the two driveways.

2.3. Pedestrian bridge over the 33rd Street driveway.

2.4. View of the 33rd Street driveway after removal of the pedestrian bridge.

2.5. Pedestrians witnessing the demolition.

2.6. View from Seventh Avenue of the demolished 31st Street driveway.

opposite

2.7. Dining Room. One particularly impressive interior was originally named the Corinthian Room but later became a Savarin Restaurant. Even in a dilapidated state, the grandeur of this room is clear.

2.8. Dining Room, from below. The plaster coffers and pilasters have been partially removed.

opposite

2.9. View of the dining room and waiting hall from the arcade.

2.10. Waiting hall facing south. The staircases which brought pedestrians
from street level to the waiting hall have been removed from the
31st Street entrance and the arcade (at left).

2.11. Corner of the waiting hall. Vertical members of
the new structure are sprouting through the floor.

2.12. The exposed steel structure of a Corinthian column
in the waiting hall.

opposite
2.13. The waiting hall seen from above.
Aaron Rose is standing above the column.

2.15. Waiting hall. The upright girders in the foreground are part of the advancing construction of the new steel floor.

2.16. The truss structure of the waiting hall ceiling.

2.17. The ceiling of the waiting hall. The plaster coffers have been removed from the right side, revealing the framework from which the coffers were suspended.

opposite   2.14. View from window level of the waiting hall.

opposite

2.18. Waiting hall in rubble.
Photographer Aaron Rose is standing
on the column shaft.

2.19. Dismantling the steel structure
of the waiting hall.

opposite

2.20. Commercial arcade seen from the waiting hall.

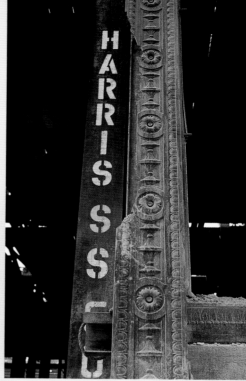

2.21. Detail of a shop front in the commercial arcade.

2.22. Steel structure of the commercial arcade. The upright red girder is new construction.

2.23. The truncated arcade and baggage courtyards looking east. The empty space in the foreground was the site of the waiting hall. The Hotel Pennsylvania stands in front of the Empire State Building.

2.24. Tracks below the southern baggage courtyard, facing east. The two converging tracks in the middle enter one tube of the crosstown tunnel.

2.28. The concourse and the Farley Post Office, seen from the Hotel Pennsylvania. The waiting hall is gone.

opposite

2.25. Roof structure of the southern baggage courtyard, facing east. The scaffolding at left covers the commercial arcade, and the end of the 31st Street driveway appears at right. Removal of the waiting hall opened a midblock shortcut.

2.26. View across the tracks toward the east end of the arcade, which has otherwise been demolished. The roof of the baggage courtyard has been removed.

2.27. Detail of the concourse roof.

2.29. Train concourse facing south. The structure of the new ceiling begins to take over.

opposite

2.30. 31st Street entrance to the concourse.

2.31. Train concourse facing south.

2.32. Ceiling of remodeled concourse.

opposite

2.33. Construction of Madison Square Garden overtakes the concourse. The remodeled train concourse is buried beneath the slab.

2.34. Concourse vaults during demolition.

2.35. Concourse vaults during demolition.

2.36. Concourse vaults during demolition, seen from Eighth Avenue. The skeletal structure of Madison Square Garden takes shape.

2.37. Seventh Avenue entrance. The skeletal form of the arena is visible through the columns.

2.38. View of the Seventh Avenue facade, the last part of the station to be demolished.

2.39. Drilling granite of the main facade.

2.40. Granite columns of the main facade.

2.41. Eagles above the station.

2.42. Transporting column drums. Most of the stone from Pennsylvania Station was dumped in the New Jersey Meadowlands.

opposite

2.43. Preparing to remove the eagles from the Seventh Avenue facade. A surveyor appears in the foreground.

2.44. Removal of an eagle.

2.45. Grounded eagles awaiting transfer.

2.46. Dismantled statuary of the main facade.

opposite

2.47. The dedicatory plaque, installed inside the main entrance, surveys the rubble.

2.48. Aerial view of Madison Square Garden under construction. The roof of the midblock drive-through entrance to the remodeled station appears at left.

opposite

2.49. Aerial view from the Hotel Pennsylvania with (from bottom to top) the Seventh Avenue entrance pavilion of the original station, the midblock driveway and entrance to the remodeled station, Madison Square Garden, and the Post Office.

The New Pennsylvania Station

Marilyn Jordan Taylor

INTRODUCTION

In less than a century New York City's remarkable Pennsylvania Station has led a tumultuous life, with the eyes of the world upon it. Opened in 1910, gone just fifty-three years later, cut off at the knees by a stroke of real estate, reduced to a subterranean existence in a loss much lamented, Penn Station now appears to be turning from legend to phoenix. Its transformation is an unusual triumph of personal persistence and civic will.

When present plans are realized, New York will see a "new" Pennsylvania Station (Fig. 3.1). More than a half-million passengers will enter and leave New York each day through an expanded and extended station that will offer clarity, comfort, and delight — words today's passengers and commuters would hardly use to describe their travel experience. A still-existing landmark will become an integral and defining element of the station. The immediate neighborhood will be engaged in station activity. The region will gain a new gateway and a sense of linkage far more extensive than even that conceived in the great transportation investments of the early twentieth century.

When the new Pennsylvania Station is completed, many people will crowd the dedication ceremony platform. Most will not have been there during the challenging years of setting the vision, engaging the concurrence of involved parties, gaining broad support, achieving funding, winning public allegiance, devising plans to implement the vision, and getting it done. I hope those who use the station, and enjoy it, will remember those who deserve the applause. It will be more than sufficient praise.

THE NEW PENNSYLVANIA STATION: THEMES

3.1 Aerial view of the new Pennsylvania Station at the James A. Farley Post Office Building, facing northwest.

The new Pennsylvania Station at the James A. Farley Post Office captures the romance of the past to create an icon of the future. A project of enormous importance to the city and the region, and to rail travel in America — a near-orphan during the years of our national affection for the car and the plane — it is intended to achieve a daunting set of objectives. Among its aims are advancing mass transportation, supporting a regional agenda, extending the public use of a landmark, establishing street-level presence and connections to the surrounding neighborhood, and lifting the spirit of travelers and passersby.

Though the project is complex, its essence is simple. The Farley Post Office, located immediately to the west of the original and current Penn Station site, will become an integral part of passenger-serving rail operations (Fig. 3.2). Three "new" and important public spaces will be added to the overall station complex: an Intermodal Hall, a Train Room, and a Platform Area. These facilities, and the circulation and support spaces related to them, will serve intercity rail travelers, passengers connecting to flights at New

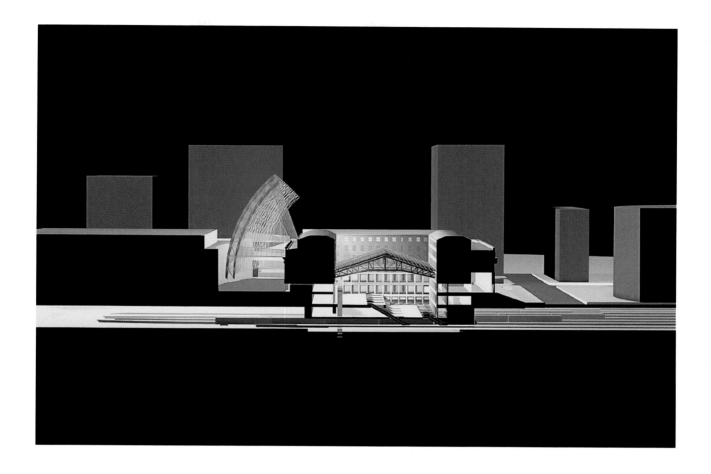

York's airports, and those commuters who find the new station areas more convenient than the existing one. Natural light will, once again, reach the subterranean platform environment. New escalators, stairs, and elevators will increase platform access by more than 30 percent, enhancing both convenience and safety for all station users. The U.S. Postal Service, occupant and owner of the Farley Building, will reconfigure and upgrade its operations within the building envelope, so that the station and its related activities can occupy approximately one-third of the building's overall space.

The past and future of Pennsylvania Station depend on an extraordinary underpinning that passes largely unseen by the crowds of people who swarm in and around this area of the city each day. Four stories (50 feet) below the street, carved into the shelf of granite that supports Manhattan, sliding beneath the subways of Seventh and Eighth Avenues, lies a transportation lifeline. Here the railroad tracks link beneath the Hudson River to New Jersey and beneath the East River to Queens, Long Island, Connecticut and points

3.2 East-west section of the new station facing north and showing, from left to right, the 1934 Post Office addition, the Intermodal Hall with enclosing shell structure, the Train Room covered by truss roof, the front wing of the Farley Building with Post Office lobby, Eighth Avenue, and Madison Square Garden on the current site of Penn Station.

beyond. Beginning just east of Tenth Avenue, these tracks fan out to encompass the entire distance between 33rd and 31st Streets, creating a station complex extending the length of two full West Side blocks. The twenty-one tracks and eleven platforms of the station are the literal and conceptual foundation of the project that will reestablish for New York a gateway that has been lacking for more than four decades.

America's historic connection between rail and mail has given Penn Station the opportunity that has been called its "second chance," the opportunity to regain the civic presence and architectural distinction appropriate to its gateway function. But this chance depends on a new joint use of the post office building sitting astride the tracks to the west of the original station. The McKim, Mead & White Main Post Office, completed in 1914, is known among New Yorkers for its monumental colonnade and stairs, its inscribed quotation about determination in the face of adversity, and its all-important function as the venue that still postmarks tax returns at midnight on April 15. The extension of passenger facilities into post office territory requires a cooperative process of establishing demising walls and extensively reconfiguring post office functions, to maintain operations and efficiency as well as to allow for future mail growth. Making the building, designed as an industrial workplace for mail carriers and postal workers, into a public destination requires changes in curbside, sidewalk, entry, and truck dock configurations, as well as a reworking of internal functions.

Perhaps, for the architects at least, the most interesting theme of the redevelopment of the Farley Building is the role that design has played, and can play, in the achievement of twenty-first-century public works. Given the broad array of actors, funding parties, governmental entities, and public opinion groups focused on this project, a bold design idea, strongly asserting the presence and the future of rail transportation, was launched. Its drama and clarity caught the public eye and helped to win the broad support the project required to overcome the funding and logistical hurdles that frequently make projects of this scale and importance impossible.

In that sense, this project provides a remarkable response to powerful questions about the opportunity and need for a well-designed infrastructure that can both serve and inspire us. One hundred years ago, at the turn of the twentieth century, the nation and its major institutions profoundly understood the need to invest in the systems and networks that would support the country's economic future. Today we face that challenge again, transformed this time to address questions of environmental responsibility and social equity as well. Is the Pennsylvania Station project an exception, or an indication that we have learned to honor the civic role, as well as the functional role, our transportation networks can play?

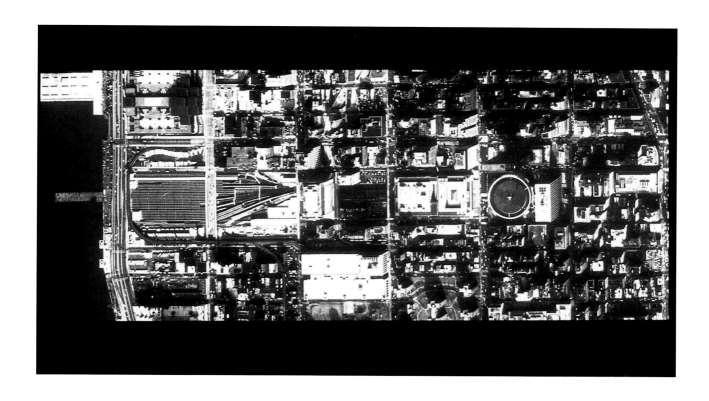

THE NEED FOR THE PROJECT

The James A. Farley Post Office occupies one of New York City's few "double" blocks, extending from 33rd to 31st Street and from Eighth to Ninth Avenue (Fig. 3.3). This defines a site 460 feet wide and 800 feet long, covering nine acres. The Farley site mirrors in its geometry the site of the original and current Penn Station. The two blocks together, combined with the intermediate avenue and areas below the adjoining streets, give the station an overall site of more than 20 acres, a fantastic resource for the city's future.

In its West Side setting, Pennsylvania Station is very different from its East Side counterpart, Grand Central Terminal. Grand Central is a terminus, bringing commuters and day-trippers directly into the center of an intensely developed urban district. Pennsylvania Station is located at the edge of midtown, surrounded by evolving industrial uses, where it serves as a stop on a through-track operation linking New Jersey to Connecticut, Washington to Boston, and, in the not-too-distant future, Newark International Airport to John F. Kennedy International Airport. Amtrak (and its new high-speed Acela service), New Jersey Transit (NJT), and the Long Island Rail Road (LIRR) all use the station's tracks and platforms. At peak periods they together operate above the theoretical capacity of the complex, serving more than 90 million passengers annually—a level of

3.3 Aerial view of the Farley site (center) bordered by Eighth and Ninth Avenues and 31st and 33rd Streets. Madison Square Garden, the circular structure, and the adjacent rectangular skyscraper occupy the site of the original Pennsylvania Station.

traffic greater than the three New York area airports combined. The number of passengers is projected to grow to more than 200 million by the year 2020, as New Jersey Transit completes major projects that will enhance access to Penn Station, as other modes of transportation reach their capacity, as airport access is initiated, and as more commuters and travelers turn to public transport.

At Penn Station, the major capacity constraints are in the number of train operations, in the overcrowded waiting and staging areas, and in the ability to move passengers quickly off the platforms. Coordinated operations, advanced train signaling systems, and the addition of East Side Access (LIRR service into Grand Central) will help Penn Station face the demands of twenty-first-century train schedules. Extending Penn Station into the Farley Building will increase platform access by more than one-third and will create the additional capacity for arriving and departing passengers this facility will demand.

Beyond capacity constraints, the worst problems of today's Penn Station lie in the limitations and confusions that are everyday experiences for all those who must use it. In recent years improvements have been, or are being, made to information systems, waiting areas for Amtrak and LIRR, concession offerings, and platform access for NJT. But these improvements, and indeed any improvements possible within the restrictive bounds of the existing station, will be inadequate to the full station future New York City requires. The skilled engineers who have extended the capacity of Penn Station to meet increasing needs recognize the limits of the present facility. New Yorkers still actively mourn the loss of the station experience they once had and know that arriving by train in a world-class city can be more than a scrambling walk through below-grade corridors. An extended Penn Station will also increase the sense of accessibility to adjoining blocks and to the areas to the west of the station; in this sense, the "new" Pennsylvania Station will be more integrally tied to its surroundings than the original Penn Station ever was.

REALIZING THE VISION

As is often the case with complex urban situations, any solution to the constraints at Penn Station requires a change to the boundaries of the problem. Such a strategy works best when founded in a vision that can evoke leadership and broad support. The source of vision and the catalyzing force behind this project is New York's senior statesman, Daniel Patrick Moynihan. Long a believer in the importance of design to the monuments and institutions of our government, to the nature of our cities, and to our national character, Moynihan played this project's most pivotal role. It was he who attracted the attention of the White House and gained the ultimate commitment of the U.S. Postal Service to a project he recognized as both critical and exemplary.

To understand the accomplishment that the new Penn Station will be, it is necessary to describe, in summary form, the recent history, the client structure, and the approval process required of the project. Achieving the redevelopment of the James A. Farley Building has entailed picking up the pieces from a previous attempt by Amtrak and LCOR, a developer skilled at public-private initiatives. Together in the early 1990s, these two parties proposed a new Amtrak station in the Farley building, but they ran into a host of difficulties including controversy with landmark officials, the lack of a real estate deal with the Postal Service, and a funding shortfall. Yet without this first attempt, Penn Station's "second chance" would not have been possible.

Resurrecting and reconfiguring the project meant creating a new entity, the Pennsylvania Station Redevelopment Corporation (PSRC), as a subsidiary of New York State's redevelopment agency, the Empire State Development Corporation (ESDC). Recognizing that the project could only be achieved with the cooperation of all levels of government (city, state, and federal), PSRC was created with a six-member board, consisting of two senior representatives from each governmental level. Board members include the U.S. Secretary of Transportation and the administrator of the Federal Railroad Administration (FRA), two senior advisers to the mayor of New York City, the chairman of ESDC, and a former deputy secretary to the governor of New York State. To ensure that the project would proceed only with the highest level of concurrence, decisions of the PSRC board must be unanimous among all members—not a quorum, not a majority vote. This mandated structure makes it necessary to attain agreement among all parties before matters are referred for board action.

Day-to-day direction of the project is placed in the hands of the officers and staff of PSRC, who in return report to the Joint Management Committee (JMC), composed of representatives of the FRA, the General Services Administration (GSA), and the U.S. Postal Service. PSRC, with the input and concurrence of the U.S. Postal Service, as building owner, engaged in a competitive selection process for the architecture/engineering team to design the project. After months of qualification rounds and interviews, amid close competition among local and international firms eager to be commissioned for such an extraordinary project, PSRC chose a team led by Skidmore, Owings & Merrill LLP. The SOM team included Arup and Parsons Brinckerhoff as engineers, Hardy Holzman Pfeiffer as preservation and civic architects, and many other team members whose combined commitment and expertise have proven necessary to the accomplishment of the design objectives.

At the direction of the JMC, the team formed working groups with Amtrak staff involved in both station operations and the implementation of Amtrak's Acela service, and with Post Office staff at the Farley Building and in the New York region. These working groups proved to be essential in defining the specifics of operations for the Farley Building and in achieving the inevitable compromises that make the project possible.

Prior to the creation of PSRC, initial public finding for the project had come from three sources: the City of New York, the State of New York, and the U.S. Government. As the project met controversy, as the requirements of the Post Office were fully defined, and as the needs of preserving a landmark were more clearly known, it became increasingly apparent that the initially allocated funds would be insufficient to the task. Much of the recent history of the project has centered on the identification and securing of additional funding sources to see the project to conclusion. The project is now funded with grants from state, federal, and city governments; bonds issued by ESDC; loans under the federal Transportation Infrastructure Financing and Innovation Act (TIFIA); private equity; and project operating revenues.

While the innovative funding package was being secured, an extensive process of public review and approval was also underway. The FRA was designated as the lead agency for the preparation of the environmental analysis, a requirement of the project; the environmental analysis was able to draw heavily on the work prepared for the earlier proposal. Because of the state and local funding, the process was crafted to comply with the requirements of state as well as federal environmental regulations. Review of changes to the landmark Farley Building was in the jurisdiction of the New York State historic preservation officer. While most members of the public were supportive of the project, controversy arose over the required modifications to the historic Post Office. Through extended studies and meetings, the controversy was ultimately resolved.

A major issue for the project arose from its one-of-a kind character. While the U.S. Postal Service agreed to share the building's volume, it had no expertise or desire to participate in rail station operation. PSRC, having come into existence to facilitate getting the project funded, designed, and built, had no mandate for an active long-term role. Amtrak and the other operating entities had capital and operating limitations that did not make it feasible to add still another facility to their constrained budgets. Retail and other revenues, while considerable, did not create enough cash flow to attract private developers to take over the station project (as, for example, at Terminal 4 at JFK International Airport, where JFKJAT, a joint venture of LCOR and Schiphol USA, has teamed with the Port Authority of New York and New Jersey to replace obsolete facilities with a new common-use terminal). The risks in building over the operating railroad and in obtaining access to the site on a predictable basis were significant hurdles to contractors interested in building the project.

A one-of-a-kind project requires a one-of-a-kind solution. PSRC, with numerous governmental, financial, and construction advisers, devised an innovative process of bidding to prequalified teams of developer/station operators. The selected team will oversee the completion of design and construction and will enter into a long-term master lease and operating agreement. Under this approach, the project will require 42 to 48 months to construct.

PROJECT OBJECTIVES

Beginning work on the design of the new Pennsylvania Station at the James A. Farley Building, SOM set four design objectives:

1) to upgrade and extend the station to serve the increased number of passengers, including commuters, local travelers, intercity travelers, and those connecting to or from the region's airports;

2) to preserve, and extend the life of, the landmark Post Office originally designed as a companion to Pennsylvania Station and now an integral part of its future;

3) to create a gateway symbolic of, and appropriate to, New York; and

4) to build on the station investment to influence both the immediate surroundings and the regional transportation system.

In setting these objectives, we were inspired by the stations of the past, most especially the two New York stations that set the stage for the twentieth century and became symbolic of the city's everyday opportunities and great moments. Upon the opening of these stations, the *New York Times* wrote in 1913,

Railway stations possess for a city something of the importance that is possessed for a country by railways themselves. It is by no means an idle or empty boast, therefore, for New York to proclaim that from today it will have in use for itself and its daily army of visitors what are beyond question two railway stations in every way superior to any other buildings for their purpose in the world.

This is a fact creditable alike to the metropolis, which has justified the erection here of structures so enormously expensive, and to the corporations, which have expended their millions in no mean and narrow spirit of hard utilitarianism, but with appreciation of *a civic duty to produce architectural monuments of a kind calculated to illustrate and to educate the aesthetic tastes of a great Nation* [italics added].

Nine months after the SOM team started design, in May 1999, President Bill Clinton came to New York to launch the project. His words reinforced the larger mission of the project. Clinton said, "Our nation is still young, and sometimes still we lose sight of the enormous value of the history that is embodied in our buildings. . . . We must do better in preserving the past, and in building new buildings and monuments that capture our vision of the future, the enduring commitment we have to our freedom, and the public space that makes community possible. . . . " He added, "if I can borrow a few words from the inscription on this building, neither snow, nor rain, nor heat, nor gloom of night could have stopped Pat Moynihan from bringing this day to pass!"

As for the senator himself, his most memorable words were said early in the project and stay with us each day. Urging speed and persistence, Moynihan wryly pointed out, to any and all involved, that "this project is a fat dolphin swimming in a sea of sharks." We learned quickly that part of our charge, regardless of context, was to make the new Pennsylvania Station inevitable.

SITE ASSETS AND RESOURCES

The block on which Penn Station sits today extends from Seventh Avenue on the east to Eighth Avenue on the west, from 33rd Street on the north to 31st Street on the south. Directly above and to the north of the station are the Madison Square Garden sports and entertainment complex and the two commercial office towers that were built when the Pennsylvania Station superstructure was demolished. Immediately east are uses of the sort that characterize much of Midtown Manhattan: offices, hotels, and shopping. To the north is the fashion/garment district, also undergoing change. To the south are residential buildings mixed with large-floorplate, commercial/industrial users, including the Morgan Building and its annex, which together with Farley serve the U.S. Postal Service operations. To the northwest lies the neighborhood known by its residents as Hell's Kitchen South, an area where changes to more intense uses extending midtown west are likely to be controversial and contested. Farther west, along the Hudson River, sits the Jacob K. Javits Convention Center, awaiting a long-planned expansion. Immediately to its south are the station yards, two blocks wide and two blocks long, a remarkable land resource for the city's future, although the nature of that future remains undecided.

Given its distance from the center of Manhattan and its lack of local public transportation, the area west of Penn Station fails to realize the coherence and quality of other New York neighborhoods. Land assembly activities, along with initial feasibility stud-

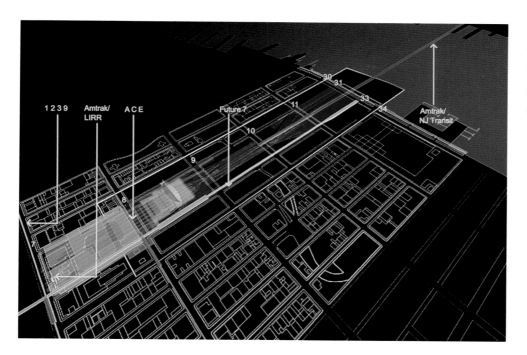

3.4 Axonometric view of the transportation resources around the Farley site, including the potential extension of the #7 subway line.

ies, are underway for many sites, and planners ranging from Phyllis Lambert of the Canadian Centre for Architecture to the New York 2012 Olympics Committee are recognizing the enormous value this district can bring in the coming decades.

Extensive regional and city transportation resources are concentrated immediately around Penn Station (Fig. 3.4). The 1, 9, 2, and 3 subways, local and express, operate in the Seventh Avenue right-of-way; there is generous access between Penn Station and the subway platforms. The A and E trains operate beneath Eighth Avenue; subway riders use constrained circulation paths at the northwest corner of the station to reach platform areas. Improvements are planned both by the Transit Authority and as a part of the proposed Penn Station project. PATH (Port Authority Trans Hudson) trains from New Jersey terminate just east of Penn Station. There is, however, no major transit connection between the station and the four major blocks of the Manhattan grid immediately to the west. A current proposal to correct this deficiency includes the extension of the number 7 subway line, which terminates at Times Square, down Eighth Avenue and west on 33rd Street to Twelfth Avenue where it would reach not only the Javits Center but also the development above the Penn Station yards.

Given the many forms of transit serving the Penn Station site and the existing investment in tracks and platforms, transportation planners have for some time been turning an envious eye toward the James A. Farley Post Office located immediately to the station's west. The building originally occupied approximately one-third of its block-long site, in

3.5 Eighth Avenue facade of the
Farley Post Office Building
designed by McKim, Mead &
White, 1914.

a classical structure designed by McKim, Mead & White as a companion piece to their
newly opened station. The building features a monumental stair that addresses Eighth
Avenue and leads patrons through a two-block-wide colonnade into a grand hall for
transacting their postal business. This decoratively elaborated hall is, however, virtually
the only part of the structure originally intended for public access. Immediately behind
the hall is a large work space, enclosed by massive spanning trusses, for sorting mail.
Wrapping the sorting hall are five stories of offices. To the west, an alley constructed
above the tracks provided access to truck docks for transferring mail.

The Post Office building was designed to create a sense of permanence and security for
postal operations, as well as to accommodate the movement of trains and the loading and
unloading of the mail. Although the building related strongly to Eighth Avenue, its
north and south facades were separated from the adjoining streets by 40-foot-wide
"moats." With the exception of Eighth Avenue, building entrances were reserved exclusively for mail and postal employees.

While the great Pennsylvania Station existed, it is likely that comparatively little public attention was paid to its quiet, dignified, but somewhat reserved neighbor to the west.
Completed in 1914 and named the Pennsylvania Terminal, the Post Office building was
designed by the station's architects as a companion piece, a proud but responsible civic
building, with no risk that it would steal the show.

McKim, Mead & White's designer, William Kendall, won the commission in a competition, and the proposal he submitted was largely, but not completely, realized as drawn. His winning entry features the two-block-long classical colonnade that creates the Post Office's front, and public, door (Fig. 3.5). This grand vestibule is reached by a flight of monumental stairs, which were widened after the competition to emphasize the great expanse of the double-block site. The vestibule is flanked on the north and south by five-story pavilions capped by "ziggurat" roofs and designed with incised, arched niches for art that unfortunately was never commissioned. The pavilions are repeated on the northwest and southwest corners of the building. Above the colonnade, which is three full stories in height, is a projecting cornice, beneath which is found the famous inscription translated from Herodotus: "Neither snow nor rain nor heat nor gloom of night stays these couriers from the swift completion of their appointed rounds." Above the cornice on all sides is an additional office floor, the fourth, identified by its punched windows. A decorative cornice caps the fourth floor. A fifth, attic story, set back from the facade, completes the building.

The projecting and decorative cornices run continuously around all four building elevations. The north and south elevations use engaged rather than freestanding columns to repeat the rhythm of the Eighth Avenue facade. These two sides of the building are set back from the street by a wide light well, or "moat," which includes a virtually continuous chest-high granite wall at its outer, public edge. The west elevation, enclosed in the building when it was extended, was more utilitarian. Its primary feature was a long canopy designed to shelter the mail and delivery trucks.

As its space needs grew, the Post Office expanded to fill the entire block with an addition completed in 1934. While the basic composition of the facades was replicated, creating powerful 800-foot-long north and south elevations, the specific detailing was modified and flattened, perhaps to reduce the cost, perhaps to respond to the Art Deco influences that were dominating public buildings being constructed at that time.

Functional modifications were also made. While the upper floors of the 1914 building wrapped the perimeter of the building and enclosed a large light-well at the building's center, the 1934 building simply included very large floor-plates on all its upper floors. Three monumental arches in the Ninth Avenue facade allowed trucks to enter the building and reach an expanded truck dock area. On 33rd Street two arches were provided for exiting trucks. Truck access to 31st Street was eliminated, but a three-arched section of facade was introduced at the juncture between the original building and its addition, where the through-block street had previously run.

Over time, additional modifications occurred. Truck docks were expanded along the western end of 31st Street by covering the moat and appropriating the use of a portion of the street and sidewalk. A second retail lobby was added on 33rd Street, bridging the moat and affording wheelchair access. Security lighting was provided, attached by mast arms to the building above the cornice level. Many internal modifications were made for postal service operations. But the two-phase landmark remains largely intact, providing a great resource for ongoing public and post office use.

The resulting structure, as used today, contains over 1.4 million square feet of space and is currently the largest general post office in the country. Here the U.S. Postal Service employs 2,400 people on a three-shift, 24-hour, 7-day schedule; these workers process over 550 million pieces of mail each year. In addition, the Eighth Avenue lobby serves 10,000 customers each day.

As an imposing and important presence in the city, the present-day Post Office has adapted its surrounding streets and sidewalks to support its function. The original truck alley is now a truck exit to 33rd Street. Trucks enter the building midblock on southbound Ninth Avenue, by using a counterflow lane to approach from the south and/or occupying multiple avenue lanes to maneuver into the building from the north. Truck docks also line the north side of 31st Street, co-opting the sidewalk and one lane for the trailers now too large to fit within the dimensions of the truck docks. Curbside parking, where allowed, is signed for post office patrons and official vehicles. These conditions effectively form a second barrier, in addition to the moat, between the Post Office structure and the city. Suited to its setting when the adjoining uses were also industrial, the building must now undergo change around its perimeter if it is to adapt to public use and become an integrated part of its neighborhood.

THE PROJECT DESIGN: SECTION AND PLANS THAT WORK

Great transportation projects are often designed in section. In the case of Pennsylvania Station, old and new, the significant opportunity in section lies in the height between the level of the surrounding streets above and the tracks and platforms below. Both the original and the new Penn Stations also take advantage of the ability to reach skyward and to bring in natural light to heighten the traveler's experience and sense of drama.

Understanding the section begins at sidewalk level along Eighth Avenue, from where today's passengers descend one level to reach the main station concourse that extends continuously between Eighth and Seventh Avenues. This concourse level, today designated as Level B (the street is known as Level C), corresponds exactly to the footprint of the departures level of the historic station. This level was once reached by a much more gracious descent into a hall inspired by the Baths of Caracalla, and thence into a train room capped by the steel and glass vaults that McKim, Mead & White used to represent new ways of enclosing dramatic public space. Sitting below Level B, but still above the tracks and the network of overhead electrification that powers the trains, is Level A. Level A originally included no major passenger processing facilities, but rather led arriving passengers back into the city; its ceiling height is low, and visual connections from space to space are very limited. Today Level A contains major circulation corridors as well as ticketing and waiting areas for the LIRR. It also includes connections to the PATH trains and the subways for all station users. The tracks and platforms form the lowest continuous station level.

As a result of this section and its history, many of the stairs from the platforms bring today's arriving passengers to Level A, while others extend directly to Level B. This introduces a significant degree of confusion so that even those users familiar with the station find themselves on a level other than the one they intended to reach. It also makes platform access difficult to control, since it is entirely possible to go "down" the "up" staircase.

3.6 East-west section through the new station and post office facing north.

3.7 North-south section through the Intermodal Hall facing east.

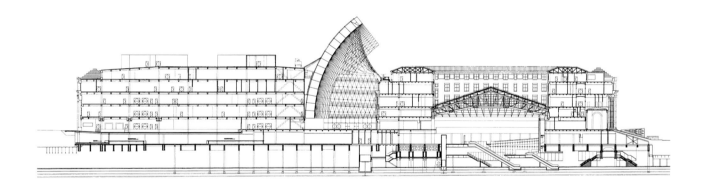

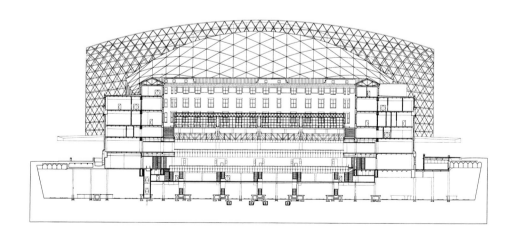

3.8 Site plan highlighting
entrances to post office facilities.

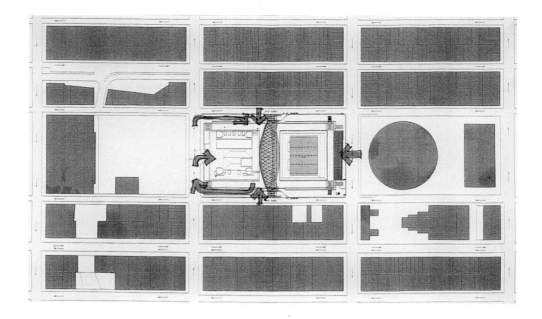

At the Farley site, the sectional condition gains even greater cogency (Figs. 3.6–7). In
this area of the city, streets rise as they extend westward, so the first floor of the Post
Office is actually one full level above Eighth Avenue but directly adjoins 33rd Street by
the time it reaches midblock on the way to Ninth Avenue. This creates two opportunities
for the new Pennsylvania Station. First, passengers can enjoy direct access without ramps
or stairs from the street into the station, something that has been lacking since the carriage drop-off areas of the historic station (later used by taxis) were demolished. Second,
the increased height between the station's street level and the platform level can be used
to provide two concourse levels, dedicated to different station functions but with a clearer relationship among levels and greater floor-to-ceiling heights than found in the existing station.

The art of transportation design rests in integrating plan with section. At the Farley
Building, it also requires integrating plan (for the station) with plan (for the postal operations). Try as we might to decipher it, there proved to be no simple east/west demar-
cation, extending from roof to basement, that would allow the two functions to co-exist.
Instead, it was necessary to discover plans of interlocking levels that gave each of the
building functions an effective new home. Although the plans were designed simultaneously, they will be described separately, for purposes of clarity.

THE POST OFFICE

Key to the reuse of the Farley Building for the U.S. Postal Service is the replacement and
upgrading of its eighty-plus existing truck docks. Over the years since 1914, as the Post
Office grew and as the shift from rail to truck occurred, its truck docks proliferated.
Today they occupy two primary locations: the western two-thirds of the first floor and

3.9 Model of the new station facing southwest. Note the ramp on 33rd Street, which provides post office vehicles with access to the loading area relocated from the side streets to the basement of the post office.

the southwestern face of the building along 31st Street. The location of several of these docks is incompatible with station use; in addition, many docks do not meet current post office or safety code standards. In the case of the 31st Street docks, they are now used for storage rather than for loading and unloading. The growth in the size of vehicles has caused the north lane of 31st Street to be occupied by post office trucks at virtually all times. The easternmost lane of Ninth Avenue has been taken over by the Post Office for counterflow movement between 31st Street and the entrance to the first floor docks. Despite these operational constraints, more than 1,100 trucks enter and leave the site on busy days.

To incorporate station functions into the Farley Building, and to allow for growth and connection to the neighborhood, the new plan removes most of these truck docks from grade and puts them in an expanded basement loading area that works with, rather than struggles against, the surrounding traffic. All post office vehicles up to 45 feet in length will be docked here, with access provided to and from Ninth Avenue by ramps that descend in the "moat" space between the sidewalks and the building facades (Figs. 3.8 and 3.9). Post office vehicles over 45 feet in length (including the intercity tractor-trailers) will continue to use a reduced and reconfigured area of the first floor, with "head-in, head-out" access from Ninth Avenue rather than the backing-in move required to reach current docks. Through these changes, the first floor can be opened to new, shared use with station functions.

The other major move of post office space is the relocation of the skylit mail sorting room, the historic core function of the facility, from its location in the original build-

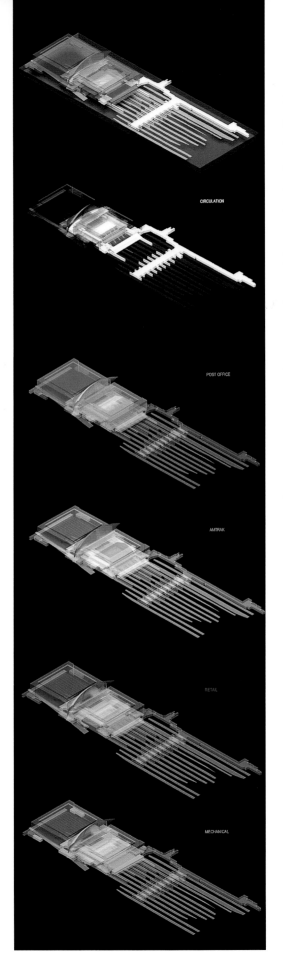

CIRCULATION

POST OFFICE

AMTRAK

RETAIL

MECHANICAL

ing to a new and upgraded area within the 1934 addition. Within the addition, new spaces will be created on the basement, first, and upper levels, to support such postal operations as mail sorting, express mail and package handling, retail support functions, mail carrier facilities for two midtown delivery zones, administrative activities, and employee amenities (Fig. 3.10). Stairs and elevators are being relocated throughout to facilitate connections among postal functions.

The facade facing Eighth Avenue, with its historic and specific inscription, will retain its Post Office identity. The monumental stairs will lead to a dramatic and monumental Post Office lobby for stamps, other retail transactions, and postmarking. The 280-foot-long hall, crowned by a vaulted and highly decorative ceiling, will be restored, as will the foyers at 33rd and 31st Streets. But rather than being an isolated destination at the top of the stairs, virtually inaccessible to the handicapped, this great hall will be tied to circulation corridors leading directly into the station and, by ramps, escalators, and elevators, to all station levels. The Post Office museum will be retained and expanded as part of the extended public levels of the building. Post office staff will continue to occupy most of the upper floors of the 1914 building, including the area behind the colonnade, which the postmaster of New York has historically called his "home."

The reconfiguration of post office facilities does not come without pain for the Post Office, whose operations must remain continuous throughout the entire construction period. In the course of relocation, however, post office spaces will be upgraded, as will major building systems including plumbing, mechanical, electrical, and information technology networks. This investment will allow the Post Office to improve its function; it may also serve other building tenants should the U.S. Postal Service decide in the future to move some of its onsite functions.

3.10 Axonometric views highlighting functional areas, from bottom to top, for mechanical, retail, Amtrak, the Post Office, and circulation, and a composite view.

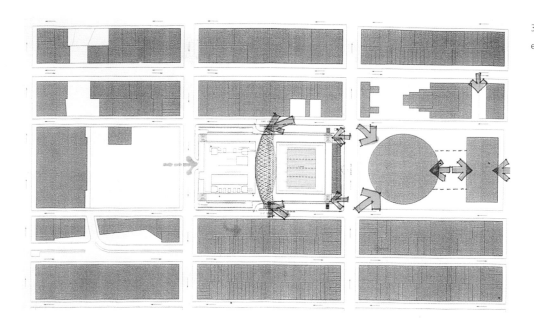

THE STATION

The relocation of post office space will allow passenger-serving station facilities to be inserted in, and threaded through, the Farley Building in a manner that meets immediate needs, allows for future growth, and promotes the long-term life of this great national landmark. A first, and very important, issue that the design team had to address was the location of the major and minor public entrances into the station complex (Fig. 3.11). The idea of altering the Eighth Avenue grand stairs to afford direct entrance for passengers was quickly discarded; in both preservation and design terms, this concept held little chance of success. In contrast, the corner pavilions at both 31st and 33rd Streets offer the potential to provide doors to station circulation, but not with the capacity, identity, and convenience the station requires. In addition, the operation of the station will require additional curbside area for drop-off and pick-up of passengers from taxis, limousines, and private vehicles. This need cannot be met on busy Eighth Avenue with its limited curb length and continuing post office use. The Eighth Avenue pavilions are suitable and convenient entries for passengers arriving at the station on foot, but alone are far from sufficient for the station's overall needs.

So the design team began looking west and found the great potential of the midblock area. As 33rd Street heads west, it rises. At the juncture between the original Post Office and its addition, the street and the first floor are on the same level. This creates an opportunity to enter the station directly from the street, without changing levels—a dramatic

3.12 First-floor plan of the new
Pennsylvania Station. Passengers
enter the Intermodal Hall from
31st and 33rd Streets at this
level, which corresponds with
the level of the post office lobby
at the top of the steps on
Eighth Avenue.

3.13 Concourse-level plan of
the new Pennsylvania Station.
Passengers approaching through
the street-level entrances in the
Eighth Avenue pavilions enter
on this level.

COLOR KEY FIGS. 3.12–15
Color indicates function
TAN =post office
BLUE =Amtrak
YELLOW =circulation
GREEN =mechanical
BLUE =retail

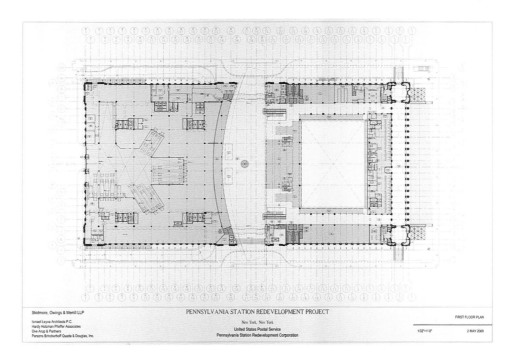

Skidmore, Owings & Merrill LLP

Ismael Leyva Architects P.C.
Hardy Holzman Pfeiffer Associates
Ove Arup & Partners
Parsons Brinckerhoff Quade & Douglas, Inc.

PENNSYLVANIA STATION REDEVELOPMENT PROJECT

New York, New York
United States Postal Service
Pennsylvania Station Redevelopment Corporation

FIRST FLOOR PLAN

1/32"=1'-0"   2 MAY 2000

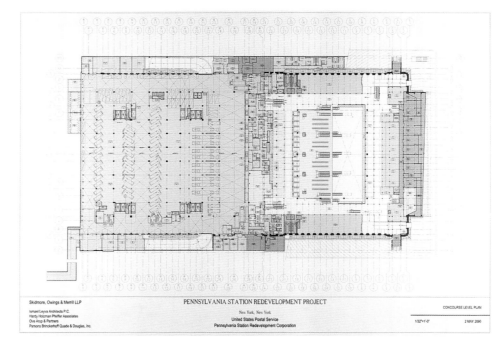

Skidmore, Owings & Merrill LLP

Ismael Leyva Architects P.C.
Hardy Holzman Pfeiffer Associates
Ove Arup & Partners
Parsons Brinckerhoff Quade & Douglas, Inc.

PENNSYLVANIA STATION REDEVELOPMENT PROJECT

New York, New York
United States Postal Service
Pennsylvania Station Redevelopment Corporation

CONCOURSE LEVEL PLAN

1/32"=1'-0"   2 MAY 2000

improvement over all existing Penn Station entrances. The relationship that has worked for post office trucks since 1914 will work for rail travelers in the future. On the 31st Street side, the street rises more gradually, leaving a distance of approximately four feet between sidewalk and station entrance. This distance will be navigated by a short flight of stairs, with elevator access for the handicapped. Each of these entrances will gain a marquee, announcing the station and sheltering passengers from the weather.

The entrances lead to the major public room of the station, the Intermodal Hall, which

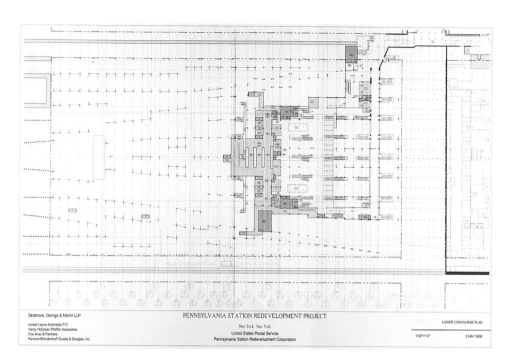

PENNSYLVANIA STATION REDEVELOPMENT PROJECT

Skidmore, Owings & Merrill LLP
Ismael Leyva Architects P.C.
Hardy Holzman Pfeiffer Associates
Ove Arup & Partners
Parsons Brinckerhoff Quade & Douglas, Inc.

New York, New York
United States Postal Service
Pennsylvania Station Redevelopment Corporation

LOWER CONCOURSE PLAN

1/32"=1'-0"   2 MAY 2000

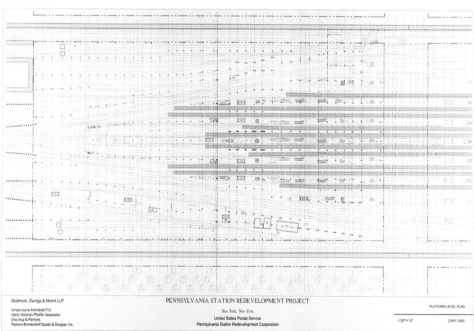

PENNSYLVANIA STATION REDEVELOPMENT PROJECT

Skidmore, Owings & Merrill LLP
Ismael Leyva Architects P.C.
Hardy Holzman Pfeiffer Associates
Ove Arup & Partners
Parsons Brinckerhoff Quade & Douglas, Inc.

New York, New York
United States Postal Service
Pennsylvania Station Redevelopment Corporation

PLATFORM LEVEL PLAN

1/32"=1'-0"   2 MAY 2000

3.14 Lower-concourse-level plan of the new Pennsylvania Station, connecting directly with the existing Penn Station facilities to the east and the Eighth Avenue subway, and corresponding with the original exit concourse.

3.15 Platform-level plan of the new Pennsylvania Station.

extends as a "through-block" space between the flanking streets (Fig. 3.12). Immediately adjoining the hall is a restaurant that overlooks the station. On the floor above are conference facilities. Extending east are two corridors lined with retail shops and leading to the Post Office lobby. On the western face are ticket and check-in facilities for airport access, as well as additional retail shops.

The functional heart of the new station lies just to the east, where the floor of the original Post Office workroom will be removed to create a new concourse for intercity travelers. Sitting two full levels above the tracks and platforms, this new Train Room includes assigned waiting areas for departing trains, with direct escalator and elevator access to the platforms when trains are called for boarding (Fig. 3.13). Ticketing and passenger amenities, as well as retail shops and a food court, line the concourse. Arriving passengers claim their checked baggage here. Passengers approaching from the Eighth Avenue pavilions enter directly onto this level.

The section of the site allows, and the realities of construction phasing mandate, the creation of a second, lower concourse level between the intercity concourse and the platforms (Fig. 3.14). Construction of this new level, at the first stage of project implementation, will protect the ongoing operation of trains below from the threat of disruption by the construction activities above. Once construction is advanced, this broad, new expanse of space, carefully fitted in among the columns and transfer girders, will give generous accommodation for commuters now required to wait on the platforms or in a low-slung corridor called the West End Concourse. Station support and baggage handling areas are also on this level, as are several concession locations to serve commuters' needs. At this level there is also a direct connection to the Eighth Avenue subway and, under Eighth Avenue, to the existing Penn Station facilities to the east.

Below the lower concourse lie the tracks and platforms, of which all but two will be directly accessible from the station at the Farley Building (Fig. 3.15). Through trains, including Amtrak, will continue to use the center tracks and platforms. NJT service will continue to operate from the platforms toward 31st Street, LIRR from those toward 33rd Street. However, in peak times and under other crowded conditions, these track and platform assignments can be modified to enhance station capacity. All passenger-serving station facilities are therefore designed for "universal use" by any of these operators.

BUILDING SERVICES AND SUPPORT

Trucks serving the station and its retail areas share access with postal service operations, but are handled in separate and secure docking facilities. Station police have locations throughout the complex.

In any major public facility serving crowds of people, the design and operation of building systems are of tremendous importance. In the case of this project, space has to be carved out of building areas to install new mechanical, electrical, plumbing, and technology systems for the station. Each system must be separate from parallel systems serving post office spaces but must occur in the least possible space to reserve maximum area for station and post office operations (see Fig. 3.10).

A significant shortfall in the existing Penn Station is the lack of quality retail stores and food concessions for passengers and commuters as well as for station employees and neighbors. The new plans provide retail space at all three station levels, located along paths of circulation and adjoining the major spaces of the station (see Fig. 3.10). In addition, the relocation of Amtrak facilities and some commuter facilities from the existing station should allow a higher level of service and amenities in expanded retail locations within that building.

In a sense, the design process for Penn Station is like solving a three-dimensional jigsaw puzzle, or building a model ship in a bottle. The fit is tight, the time to implement it is short, the demands of an operating railroad environment are great, and the compromises made by each party are real, though thankfully, small. Despite these conditions, the plans the design team has prepared create a new series of public spaces and support areas that together allow the Post Office and the station to move into the twenty-first century without the embarrassment they felt at the end of the twentieth.

DESIGN INTENTIONS: A GREAT CIVIC BUILDING

When New Yorkers became aware of the project to redevelop the Farley Building, many voices called for a "restoration" of the original Pennsylvania Station, although on a different site. The design team took a different direction, following the spirit rather than the literal intent of this sentiment. While we were, and are, keenly committed to the underlying principles of the station's classical architecture, we felt that a respectful but slavish re-creation was not what the project, or the future, required. We sought instead a design that would address the twenty-first century, and the needs of travelers today, just as the original landmark had so successfully addressed its time (Fig. 3.16).

The new Pennsylvania Station at the Farley Building is a modern expression of timeless classical principles. The qualities of the existing landmark are celebrated. New elements are woven around, and into, the existing structure, highlighting the new uses and the forward-looking changes to the building and its addition. Three new public spaces are added to the previously public but insular Post Office lobby. Architecture old and new links these four public spaces together.

These changes are dramatically expressed in the new Intermodal Hall, a space created in the zone between the 1914 building and its reconfigured annex (Figs. 3.17 and 3.18).

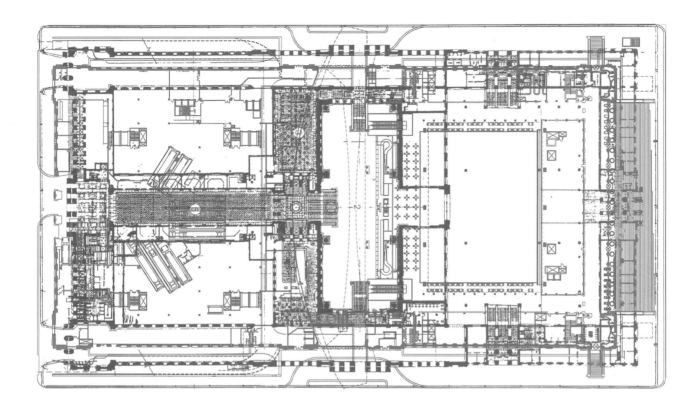

3.16 Plan overlays of the new Pennsylvania Station in red and the original station in gray.

opposite

3.17 The Intermodal Hall and shell structure from 33rd Street, detail of model. The shell structure rises 150 feet, the height of McKim's waiting hall. The soaring west side of the shell structure is made of a double shell, each with a different curvature and shape. It is closed off by a glass skylight that extends from the Farley Building to the curving space frame.

To create this space from an area currently occupied by truck docks, the original, classically detailed, west wall of the 1914 building will be revealed. To its west, a new wall, gently elliptical in plan, will rise, carving the new and inspiring hall out of formerly utilitarian areas. The hall will address both 33rd and 31st Streets with glass curtain walls, affording generous access and great visibility to the station functions within.

The enclosure of the Intermodal Hall grows out of its plan. A double-layer shell of steel and glass extends the form of the new elliptical wall, arcing to a height of 150 feet above the hall's floor and gently tilting eastward. Proudly present by day and glowing into the sky at night, this shell is both a gesture of respect for the Post Office and a welcome to the traveling public arriving and departing New York City (Figs 3.19 and 3.20). The geometry of the shell is derived from classical principles, defined from a point of origin beneath Eighth Avenue at the center of the track and platform complex (Figs 3.21 and 3.24). This same geometry causes the shell to project out beyond the landmark facades at the midblock entry points, signaling the presence of the station and its entrances in the surrounding urban form.

While the enclosure of the Intermodal Hall will be visible along the cross-town streets, it will not be seen from the Post Office steps or even from viewpoints across Eighth

3.18 Eighth Avenue elevation of the Farley Building, showing the train platforms below, the new street-level entrances to the station in the pavilions flanking the staircase, and the soaring shell structure.

3.19 Model of the new Pennsylvania Station, facing southwest.

opposite
3.20 Interior view of the Intermodal Hall and shell structure facing south from the 33rd Street entrance. The view shows the restored west facade of the Farley Building at left.

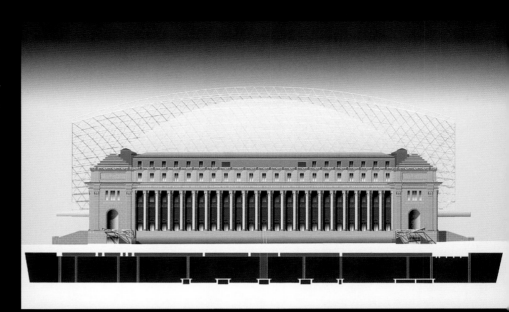

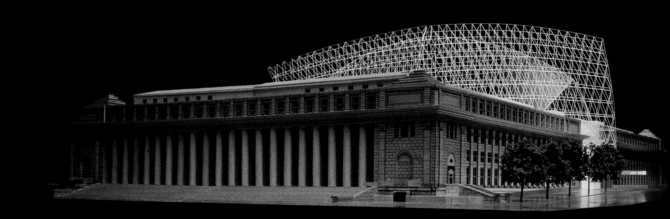

3.21 Diagram of the geometry
of the shell structure. The structure has a double shell; the inner
shell is green, the outer shell,
blue. The circles generated the
arcs of the double shell in plan
and section.

3.22 Diagram of the geometry
of the shell structure in plan in
relation to the Farley Building.

3.23 Diagram of the geometry
of the shell structure in section
in relation to the Farley
Building.

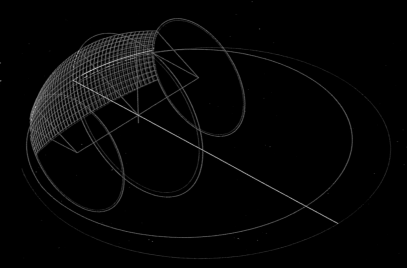

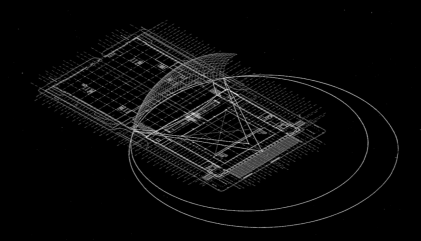

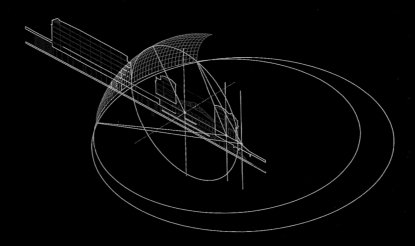

Avenue opposite the Post Office's monumental facade. Yet its compelling scale and lightness of structure will conspire to create a space different from any other in the city today. Its modernity will be a foil to the remarkable, and legitimate, restoration of Grand Central Terminal and to the other station spaces in the Penn Station complex.

Immediately to the east of the Intermodal Hall, positioned strategically above the platforms, is the Train Room (Figs 3.25–28). While the Intermodal Hall rises toward the sky, the Train Room reaches down toward the granite and the rails. The removal of the floor of the mail sorting room creates a dramatic space 80 feet high. Three original industrial trusses span the room and reveal the building's past, but the roof enclosure is simplified from its hipped configuration to a simple gabled form. The roof itself is composed of glass and lightweight steel, to admit an increased amount of natural light. Through the roof, natural light will fall to the main concourse, the lower concourse, and the platforms, due to the stepped section created by the station plans. The section also allows passengers on both concourses to see the trains pulling into the station, reclaiming one of the most exciting features of its McKim, Mead & White predecessor. Consistent with today's codes, however, the view will be through a glass enclosure that separates the track and platform level from the inhabited spaces above.

The eastern wall of the Train Room features a media wall designed to give passengers, well-wishers, meeters and greeters, and other users of the station a vast array of information including real-time train and plane schedules, travel and business information, news and civic exhibitions, and advertising. The media wall, a 45-foot by 180-foot display visible from the main and lower concourses as well as from the first floor and the sec-

3.24 Wire-frame drawing of the new Pennsylvania Station from 33rd Street, facing south.

181

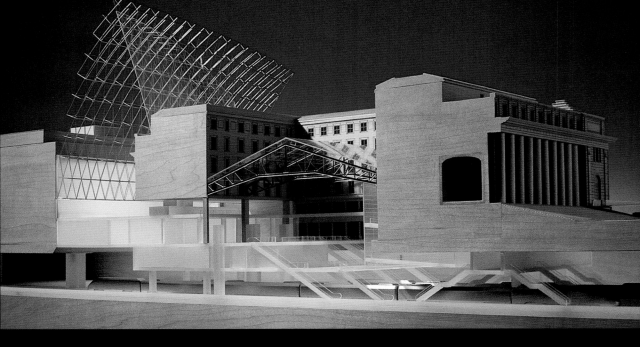

3.25 Sectional view of study model facing northwest.

3.26 Interior view of the mail sorting room in the Farley Building revealing the original skylight and truss, January 4, 1913.

3.27 Interior view of the Train Room from concourse level, facing northeast. Escalators lead from the concourse to the lower concourse and train platforms. A media wall encloses the east side of the Train Room. A window at the foot of the media wall folds down to become part of the floor and creates a visual connection between the Train Room and the platforms, as in McKim's train concourse. Retail shops border the concourse.

opposite

3.28 Interior view of the Train Room and the original truss enclosed by a new glass skylight.

Pixel by Pixel '99

3.29 View from a train platform into the Train Room.

ond floor conference facilities, offers a technological edge and a currency to the station and its users.

At the new Penn Station, the boarding and alighting platforms are treated as an integral part of the station, not as its basement (Fig 3.29). For departing passengers, natural light will guide their descent from the waiting area to the train. For arriving passengers, the effect will be more dramatic. Although natural light will reach only a small portion of the platform, its presence will create a sense of place and orientation as passengers disembark. Passengers will quickly discover that the light indicates the location of the Farley Building above and, with it, the baggage claim area, the station exits, and the taxi stands and other transportation by which they will complete their arrival in New York.

The design of the new Penn Station encompasses much more than just its major spaces. As connections are made from space to space, the intentional juxtaposition of old and new continues. The rooms, corridors, and other spaces that retain their historic detailing largely intact are preserved, with minor missing details replaced. When previous changes have removed the past, or where new spaces reveal surfaces not seen before, contemporary materials and details are used. Similarly, the history of the building and its new uses are carefully interwoven. Beneath the original trusses, the patterns in the new terrazzo floors express the position and alignment of the tracks below, unseen in the days of post office operation, but now made visible.

DESIGN INTENTIONS: A LANDMARK PRESERVED

One of the most exciting aspects of this project is the opportunity it presents to reuse a large and significant landmark building, also designed by McKim, Mead & White, as the twenty-first-century extension of the station complex they helped to create some ninety years ago. That station became famous around the world—and thus larger than its mere physical extent—not only as New York's gateway but also as a backdrop for offering welcome and saying good-bye, as a movie set, and as an evocative symbol of the great moments of the first half of the twentieth century. Its replacement, a virtual basement, may be functional but certainly lacks such resonance.

The challenge for the design team was to learn the past, to evoke its personal and civic qualities, but not to repeat it. Equally important was to understand the qualities of the Farley Building and to modify its use respectfully, but with an eye to the future.

Years of use and accretion have taken a toll on the Farley Building, much of which the new design will reverse. The building will be cleaned, and missing details, especially evident in the deteriorated decorative cornice, will be replaced. The obtrusive security lighting will be removed. The beautiful Eighth Avenue lobby and vestibules will be fully restored (Fig. 3.30).

Subtle changes will enhance the public character of the building. New doors will be carefully fitted into the base of the Eighth Avenue pavilions, giving passengers on foot a direct route to the main concourse of the new Train Room. Small glass and metal canopies will shelter those new entrances. Narrowed moats will allow the sidewalks along 33rd and 31st Streets to be widened for the increased pedestrian movement that the station will bring. Passenger drop-off and pick-up areas will be inserted midblock on each of the cross-town streets, and curb-cuts will be introduced to create sheltered areas in which passengers can alight from, or board, taxis and private vehicles.

It is at these new midblock entrances that the design of the project calls for a major, highly visible modification to the historic post office structure. This particular design direction caused considerable consternation on the part of landmark officials understandably startled by its boldness.

In the design, the major street-level space of the station extends continuously from 33rd Street to 31st Street. This space, the Intermodal Hall, welcomes passengers into the station and gives them a sense of both awe and orientation. To do so, it rises dramatically above the continuous datum of the Post Office cornice, recalling in approximate size and location (though not architectural expression) the volume of the classical ticketing hall of the original Pennsylvania Station to the east. In addition, in order to create visibility into the station and to provide generous access and egress, two 65-foot segments of the historic masonry elevation, one on each cross-town street, will be removed and replaced by a new facade of glass and metal (Figs. 3.31 and 3.32). The removal of this portion of the 1934 addition, necessary to the new transportation use of the building, reveals the presently encased west elevation of the 1914 building. To the designers, this had the benefit of revealing the two-part history of the building, a fact now generally obscured. But it also created a design dilemma: how to replace the former elevation, demolished in 1934, to bind the buildings together.

3.30 The lobby of the Farley Building Post Office.

The architectural design of the Intermodal Hall—its roof enclosure, the new facades, the new interior walls, and the canopies providing shelter over the station entrances—requires the simultaneous and integrated solution of all the pieces being newly inserted into the historic fabric of the landmark building. Our approach was to design these elements in clear and dramatic contrast to the classical vocabulary, solidity, and gravity of the landmark. The sweeping double-shell roof lifts gracefully above the hall as a lightweight structure of metal and glass; it tips toward Eighth Avenue and the 1914 building. The geometry of the shell causes it to project beyond the perimeter of the building, over the moat and the station entrance, where it interrupts the long, classical continuity of the Post Office facade and marks the presence of the station in the city. The facade, like the shell, is composed of metal and glass; it folds down from the shell to create the station entrance. A cantilevered glass canopy protects the entrance.

The design team defined and investigated many alternatives before coming to our recommended direction. These alternatives included trapping the shell within the masonry facades (too explosive!), allowing the shell to slice through the masonry facades which were otherwise kept in place (too strange!), and keeping the masonry area between the

cornices but changing the area below to accommodate station entrance requirements (too architecturally illiterate!). Slowly and methodically, through a process of representing alternatives in computer projection from the viewpoint of travelers approaching and arriving at the station, the answer became clear to nearly everyone. Not only was alteration required, but also the most extensive alteration had preferred results for both the station and the landmark.

This decision narrowed the options for the newly revealed west facade of the 1914 building. As described above, each of the four corner points of the 1914 Post Office was architecturally defined by a four-story stone pavilion, which was capped by a stepped pyramidal roof. The west-facing facades of the two midblock pavilions, as well as much of the western facade, were destroyed when the 1934 Annex was built. As part of the addition will now be removed, the missing facade must be replaced. It would be possible, if of dubious historic content, to restore the façade to its original appearance, modifying it only as the change in function necessitates. However, it is also possible to treat the wall as a new element, recalling its predecessor in form and scale but built of modern materials like those used in the other new station elements. After much discussion with land-

3.31 View of the two arched bays on 33rd Street between the 1914 Post Office, at left, and the 1934 addition, at right. This part of the wall be replaced by the entrance to the new station and Intermodal Hall.

THE NEW PENN STATION

mark officials, the latter approach was selected. The east wall of the Intermodal Hall will feature the long-span transfer girder concealed until now and a newly finished wall of zinc-coated copper, articulated to give scale and proportion—clearly an indication of the future, not a reversion to the past (Fig. 3.33).

In its public information meeting, the New York City Landmarks Commission praised the project for its illustration of what preservation of twentieth century landmarks should mean for the twenty-first century.

DESIGN INTENTIONS: PENN STATION AND THE CITY

The historic Pennsylvania Station is celebrated as a proud classical landmark, but it was not exactly a deeply integrated urban building. Its massive presence was announced by grand, projected, columned, and pedimented entrances on Seventh Avenue, 31st and 33rd Streets. Pedestrians might enter at these entrances, but passengers arriving by carriages, with the trunks and luggage characteristic of travel, were sent down ramps, perpendicular to the cross-town streets, to entrances below grade. The experience before them, in the towering classical ticketing hall and then in the brilliantly structured concourse, was awe-inspiring but largely internal. The "show" was inside, in the interaction among passengers and in the highly visible, and audible, arrival and departure of the trains.

In the course of the design phase, the design team met more than a few people who remembered the experience of the station. Some said they actually cut through it in the morning, on their way to work, simply for the pleasure of the passage.

The extended station in the Farley Post Office faces the challenges of the building's serious architectural demeanor but still possesses the opportunity to express its significance and to engage the city around it. Critical to this opportunity is the fact that, at last, this formerly industrial sector of the city is finding its moment for redefinition. The plan for the station seizes this future, knowing that while it may take some time to realize, the wait will have been worth it.

The first strategy for creating an urban station lies within the Post Office site. The current Post Office configuration, with its truck dock at grade, poses a significant physical impediment to western movement within the site. By removing the majority of truck docks to the new basement loading facility, the design opens the near-term potential for through-block circulation in an east-west, as well as a north-south, direction. This cross-axial organization, implied in the design, recalls the 1914 station plan and allows the new station, in the future, to claim entry and presence on Ninth Avenue as well as on the three other coordinate locations. So if the U.S. Postal Service should at a future time decide to relocate tractor-trailer operations and/or any related facilities, the current investment in

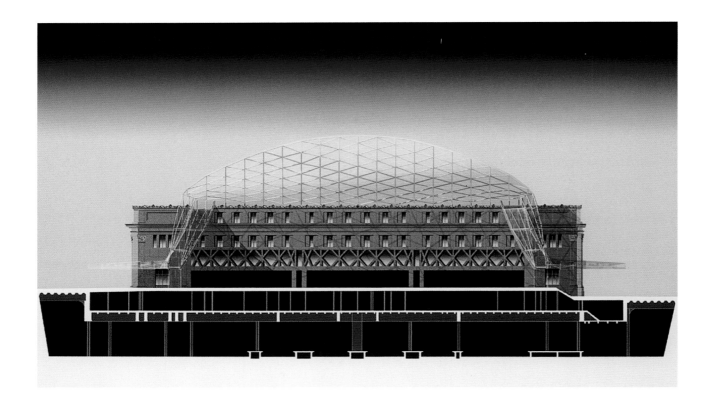

3.33 North-south section
through the Intermodal Hall,
facing east, revealing the long-
span transfer girder of the Farley
Building.

the building is ready to be more fully realized. Passengers would then approach the station from all four of its urban faces, enjoying the new interconnection to the west as well as increased opportunities for shopping, entertainment, and station amenities.

A relocation of some or all of the postal service operations at the Farley Building could lead to even more exciting changes for the neighborhood. Up to one million square feet of additional space would be available for uses responsive to the emerging character of the district. This future only necessitates finding a new home for those postal service functions that must remain in the immediate vicinity of the site. In addition, the presence here of such broad transportation resources may well argue for an up-zoning—increase in the allowable development—which could in turn entail a transfer of development rights away from the landmark site to receiving sites linked by the below-grade train right-of-way. This could catalyze major change to the area and would reinforce its role at the focal point of local, regional, national, and international transportation access.

Four potential design visions for the future of this pivotal area of Manhattan—one of its few remaining land resources—were proposed in a provocative and intriguing competition sponsored in 1999 by Phyllis Lambert and the International Centre for Canadian Architecture (IFCCA). Lambert saw the potential of the underutilized railroad yards to the west of Midtown Manhattan not only in terms of their urban merit but also in terms of their philosophical intrigue for four leading architects invited to create design propositions for a new urban future on the rail yard site. The winning submission was that of New York architect Peter Eisenman who invited SOM to collaborate with him in a sweeping mixed-use proposal encompassing incremental development and new civic venues as well as extensive parkland (Fig. 3.34).

Together with Eisenman, we extended the site, annexing the existing station, the development above it, and the adjoining blocks to the specified competition site. This we did in the firm belief that the future holds no viable solution independent of the means of transportation, and of the resulting networks of pedestrian movement that facilitate their existence. We then proceeded to devise a new urban framework, one in which major generators of public place and meaning (a new Madison Square Garden, a stadium, a convention center extension, and a media center) are enfolded in high-density, largely low-rise urban community. Unlike today's urban redevelopment schema, which are too often characterized by a patronizing and exclusive overview, this framework can allow the participation of all interested owners, large and small, in the future of the neighborhood. The public sector provides connections, the private sector provides the venues of attraction and definition, and individual investors complete the framework with live/work locations that engage the new in the surrounding districts. Atop the complex is an extraordinary park, an open space at roof level, connecting midtown to the Hudson River and giving all city residents—not just those who live and work here—access to light, air, and spaces of relaxation and repose. The result is an integral city sector that encourages assembly and movement but that offers incremental investment and common amenity. Its utopian message is appropriate to the demands on New York to define an urban future, regardless of who the architects and urban designers may ultimately be. The need for urban vision is more imperative than ever, and transportation investment is critical to the accomplishment of this vision.

However, a more immediate possibility awaits. This vision relies on a commitment to the region and its interlocked transportation resources. It evokes a future enviable among all American, and some international, cities. This vision sees airports as important and integral elements of regional infrastructure, not as runways with related passenger and cargo facilities relegated to the periphery of urban settings.

In this vision the political boundaries of New York give way, in transportation terms at least, to the experience and everyday life of the New York region (Fig. 3.35). The extended, new Pennsylvania Station is easily reached not only by subways from all city origins, commuter trains from outlying suburbs, and intercity trains but also by airport connections, trains from Newark, express subways from LaGuardia, and one-seat rides

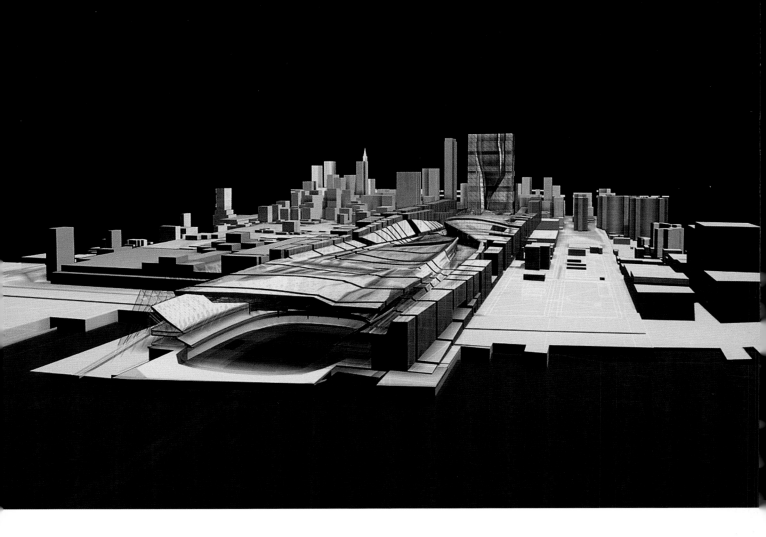

3.34 Model of project by Peter Eisenman with SOM for the Westside Competition, encompassing the rail yards west of Penn Station, facing east, 1999.

from JFK. These trains utilize Penn Station not as the end of the line but as a through-service stop, connecting suburb to suburb, city to city, airport to airport, mail sender to mail recipient. The Penn Station gateway gains not only its lost meaning but also its focal future in a multivariant network of twenty-first century urban life.

The urban vision for the new Penn Station is tripartite, merging strategies for onsite circulation, nearby development, and regional transportation investment, to win public support to realize its extraordinary potential as station, memory, and dream.

THE PASSENGER'S EXPERIENCE

Let's take a moment to describe the experience of passengers at Penn Station just a few years from now. If you are departing New York for Washington or Boston, you'll be coming to Penn Station to catch a high-speed train that will take you from city center to city center in less cumulative time, and perhaps with a better level of service, than a comparable air flight. Should you arrive at the station by taxi, a porter will check your bag or

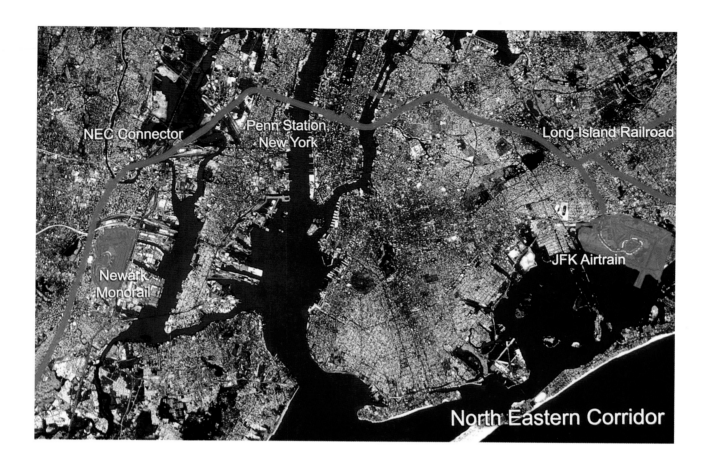

assist you in bringing it to the waiting area for your train. Should you come by subway, or by commuter train, you will transfer through the main concourse, enjoying the natural light as well as the certainty that you will soon see your train arrive on the station tracks below. If your immediate destination is one of the New York airports, you can use the Intermodal Hall to check in for your flight and forward your bags to your ultimate destination. You will enjoy the confidence that your travel to the airport will be quick and reliable, unfettered by bridge, tunnel, or highway congestion.

While you are waiting, you can remain in close touch with the status of your train; with world events such as news, financial reports, and human interest stories; and with other projected data—all available on a series of giant screens next to, and visible from, all areas of the Train Room. Should you prefer to relax, you can shop, grab a snack, or dine at a restaurant while waiting for your departure. Lounges for premier-class train passengers and frequent travelers are available, adjoining the departures zone. If you have additional time, you may choose to visit the Post Office museum, to buy stamps, or simply to enjoy the historic Post Office lobby.

3.35 Aerial view of the metropolitan region showing the Northeastern Corridor (NEC) rail linkages between Newark Airport, Pennsylvania Station, and Kennedy Airport.

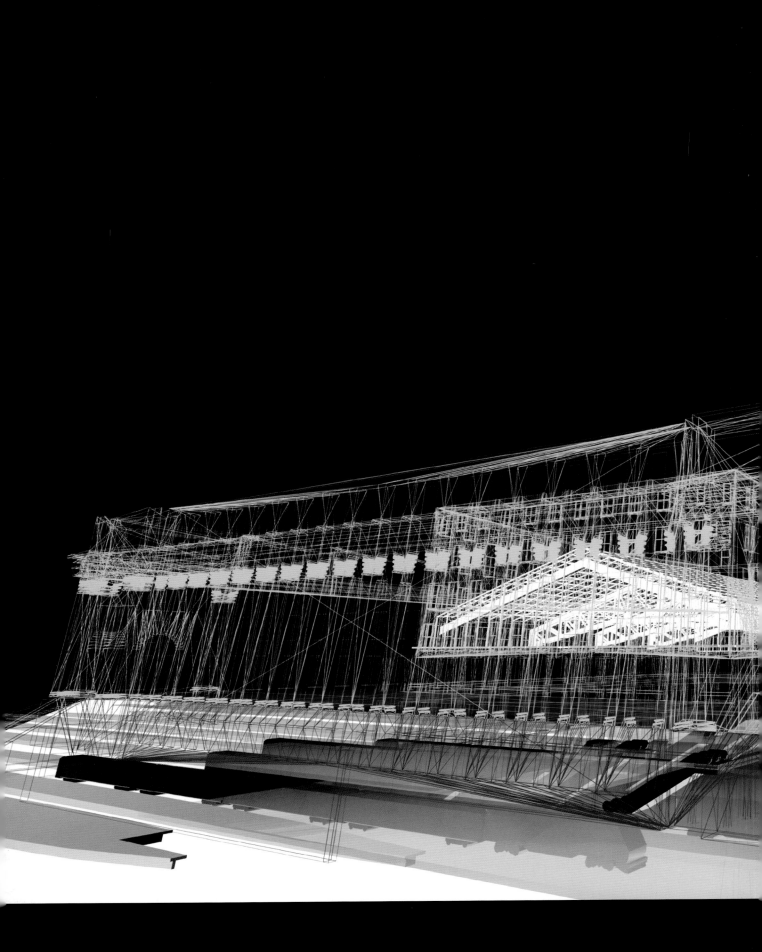

3.36 Wire-frame drawing of the new Pennsylvania Station from 33rd Street, facing southeast.

If you are arriving in New York City, you will be greeted by natural light and a clear path to the station services that can help speed you to your final destination. If you checked a bag on the train, you can claim it here and then be guided to convenient taxi, limousine, and subway access. You will also be able to transfer from intercity and commuter trains to the airport access services. There will be designated areas where meeters and greeters can find their awaited guests and family members. Attended taxi stands at 31st and 33rd Street entrances will provide safe and assisted transfer to vehicles for the last leg of your journey.

In the new Penn Station, travelers will regain a sense of civic dignity, the pleasure of travel, the meaning of arrival and departure, and the glory of America's most influential city (Fig. 3.36). The spacious halls, the convenience of choice, the setting for both an everyday experience and an extraordinary one, will all be here, once again reveling in New York's position at the center of the world and revealing the role of its great Pennsylvania Station.

THE NEW PENNSYLVANIA STATION AT THE FARLEY BUILDING

CLIENT: Pennsylvania Station Redevelopment Corporation, United States Postal Service.
PROJECT TEAM:
DESIGN PARTNER: David Childs
PLANNING PARTNER: Marilyn Taylor
PROJECT ARCHITECT: Ross Wimer
PROJECT MANAGER: Christopher McCready
SENIOR TECHNICAL COORDINATOR: Kevin Peters
DESIGN TEAM: Anthony Pascocello, Michael Fei, Nazila Duran, Tran Vinh,
    Mi Yeon Kim, Scott Duncan, Carolyn Bemis
PROJECT ASSISTANT: Ingo Jung
STRUCTURAL AND MECHANICAL ENGINEERS: Ove Arup and Partners,
    Parson Brinkerhoff Quade & Douglas
HISTORIC PRESERVATION ARCHITECT: Hardy Holzman Pfeiffer Associates

Notes

1. Letter from Samuel Rea to Bert Hanson, president of the Municipal Art Society of New York, December 6, 1910, Hagley Museum and Library, Acc. 1807, Box 141, Folder 5.

2. "Past Wonders; Those of To-Day," *The Evening Sun*, February 3, 1912. The professor was A. D. F. Hamlin.

3. The Pennsylvania Railroad operated four ferry lines from the Jersey City Terminal; one line went to Brooklyn, the others to Manhattan docks at 23rd Street (following the closure in 1897 of the ferry line to 34th Street), Desbrosses Street, and Cortlandt Street. On the Pennsylvania Railroad's ferry service, see Brian J. Cudahy, *Over and Back. The History of Ferryboats in New York Harbor* (New York, 1990).

4. The Pennsylvania Railroad modernized its fleet of seventeen ferryboats in the 1890s by installing electric lights, improved heating, and upper decks to facilitate the embarkation of passengers from elevated railroad platforms.

5. On train speeds, see Carl Condit, *The Port of New York*, vol. 1, *A History of the Rail and Terminal System from the Beginnings to Pennsylvania Station* (Chicago/London, 1980), 162.

6. [Pennsylvania Railroad Company], *The New York Improvement and Tunnel Extension of the Pennsylvania Railroad* (Philadelphia, 1910), 6.

7. I could not locate Rea's original report and relied on the summary in H. W. Schotter, *The Growth and Development of the Pennsylvania Railroad Company* (Philadelphia, 1927), 271–74. For a discussion of Rea's report, see Condit, *Port of New York*, vol. 1, 264–65.

8. On May 7, 1903, New York State passed legislation outlawing the running of steam engines in Manhattan. The legislation ratified decisions already made by the Pennsylvania and New York Central Railroads to electrify their lines.

9. On Lindenthal's North River Bridge, see Henry Petroski, *Engineers of Dreams* (New York, 1995), 130–58; and Condit, *Port of New York*, vol. 1, 256–58.

10. On the New Jersey terminals on the west shore of the Hudson River, see Condit, *Port of New York*, vol. 1, chap. 5.

11. On experiments with railroad electrification, see Condit, *Port of New York*, vol. 1, chap. 6, "The Background to the New York Electrifications," originally published as "The Pioneer Stage of Railroad Electrification," *Transactions of the American Philosophical Society*, vol. 67, part 7 (1977); and William D. Middleton, *When the Steam Railroads Electrified* (Milwaukee, 1974).

12. The Pennsylvania Railroad formed a subsidiary corporation on December 11, 1901, to build the New York extension, at which time Cassatt presented a map of the chosen route. It was left to a board of engineers, formed shortly thereafter, to work out the technical details. After several name changes, the corporation was known as the Pennsylvania Tunnel and Terminal Railroad Company.

13. For a precise description of the route, including the track mileage of each section, engineers and contractors, construction methods and costs, see *The Pennsylvania Railroad Company. Corporate, Financial and Construction History of Lines Owned, Operated and Controlled to December 31, 1945*, vol. 2, Lines East of Pittsburgh (New York, 1946), 3–43.

14. On the New York Connecting Railroad and the Hell Gate Bridge, see William D. Middleton, *Manhattan Gateway. New York's Pennsylvania Station* (Waukesha, Wisconsin, 1996), 73–88; and Petroski, *Engineers of Dreams*, 182–91.

15. *The New York Improvement and Tunnel Extension of the Pennsylvania Railroad* (Philadelphia, August 1910), 4. The exact cost of the extension as of December 31, 1910, was $112,965,415, according to the annual report of the Pennsylvania Railroad; see Schotter, *Growth and Development of the PRR*, 318. Including the New York Connecting Railroad, the figure climbed to $150 million.

16. "The Immense 'Culebra Cut' in the Heart of New York City," *Harper's Weekly*, October 20, 1906, 1493.

17. Cited by Middleton, *Manhattan Gateway*, 85. The comment refers to both the New York Extension and the Connecting Railroad.

18. The financial condition of the company is discussed in Condit, *Port of New York*, vol. 1, 268, and Schotter, *Growth and Development of the PRR*, 301–2.

19. Among the most informative newspaper articles is Arthur B. Reeve, "The Romance of Tunnel Building," *World's Work*, 13/2 (December 1906), 8338–51.

20. The only changes in the tunnels came in the early 1930s, when the track bed was lowered eight feet to accommodate the new catenary. The Board of Engineers approved the contract for construction of the Hudson River Tunnel with the O'Rourke Engineering Construction Company for $7.3 million on March 10, 1904; see The New York Public Library, Penn Central Records, Astor, Lenox and Tilden Foundations, Manuscripts and Archives Division, Penn Central Transportation Company Records (hereafter abbreviated as NYPL, Penn Central Records), Box 90. Federal transportation officials have recently raised fire and safety concerns about the ninety-year-old tunnels, in particular the inadequacy of escape routes, access for firefighters and paramedics, and ventilation systems; see Dean Murphy, "As New Penn Station Proceeds, Officials Say Tunnel Problems

Tempt Fate," *New York Times*, December 10, 2000, B7; and Dean Murphy, "Penn Station Needs Millions for Repairs," *New York Times*, December 19, 2000, B1.

21. Samuel O. Dunn, "The Problem of the Modern Terminal," *Scribner's Magazine* 52/4 (October 1912), 425.

22. Letter from Samuel Rea to Ivy Lee, January 11, 1907, Hagley Museum and Library, Acc. 1810, Box 149, Folder 22.

23. The sites set forth in Rea's report of 1892 were as follows: Christopher Street, just south of Washington Square; near Madison Square; beside the docks at 42nd Street; and Madison Avenue and 38th Street. Each variant of Lindenthal's North River Bridge located the station on different sites between 23rd and 57th Streets, all on the west side. In the last iteration of the bridge, the station was located at Seventh Avenue and 36th Street, not far from the eventual site.

24. William McAdoo resumed construction of the Haskin Tunnel in 1901 and began building an underground rapid transit system in lower Manhattan. The tunnels were put in service in 1909, and the 33rd Street stop opened in March 1910, half a year before Penn Station was operational. On the Hudson and Manhattan Railroad Company, see Clifton Hood, *722 Miles. The Building of the Subways and How They Transformed New York* (Baltimore/London, 1993), 145–50; and Brian Cudahy, *Rails under the Mighty Hudson: The Story of the Hudson Tubes, the Pennsy Tunnels and Manhattan Transfer* (Brattleboro, Vermont, 1975).

25. The top of the railroad's tunnels in Manhattan had to be at least nineteen feet below the street surface so as not to interfere with the future construction of subways. The tunnels were considerably deeper. Rea's opposition to a tunnel in the 1890s was based on his assessment that conditions in the Hudson River "would not permit the construction of a tunnel on admissible gradients for heavy traffic and for fast trains, which of course would be essential requisites" (cited by Condit, *Port of New York*, vol. 1, 258). On the depths and gradients of the tunnels, see Charles Raymond, "The New York Tunnel Extension and Connections" (Paper 1150 of a special issue on the New York Tunnel Extension of the Pennsylvania Railroad), *Transactions of the American Society of Civil Engineers*, LXVIII (Sept. 1910), 22–23.

26. Fritz Steele, "The Deserted Village . . . A Desecration," *New York Herald*, May 10, 1903, 6. My discussion of the Tenderloin is informed by the seminar paper of Hannah Goldberg.

27. Parkhurst's cicerone in the neighborhood was Detective Charles Gardner, who published an account of their joint findings, *The Doctor and the Devil: A Startling Expose of Municipal Corruption* (New York, 1894).

28. Letter from Augustus Howard Ivins, president, The A.H. Ivins Co. Real Estate, to Samuel Rea, December 13, 1912, Hagley Museum and Library, Acc. 1807, Box 148, Folder 3.

29. Steele, "The Deserted Village."

30. "It is the understanding that immigrants will be handled at Jersey City and that no provisions are to be made for them at the New York Terminal." Hagley Museum and Library, Acc. 1810, Box 146, Folder 5, "Notes on Conferences on New York Terminal Station Facilities, Held Feb. 13, 1908, in New York City and Feb. 25, 1908, at Broad Street Station, Philadelphia," 2.

31. "Landmarks in the Famous Home of Vice and Blackmail Passing into History with the Building of the Pennsylvania Railroad Station," *New York Herald*, May 10, 1903, 6.

32. "Pennsylvania's New York Station," *Architectural Record* 27 (June 1910), 519.

33. The railroad bought land through the Stuyvesant Real Estate Company, a subsidiary incorporated in November 1901, one month before the railroad's plans were made public.

34. On the terms of sale, see the acquisition records of the Stuyvesant Real Estate Company, NYPL, Penn Central Records, Boxes 13 and 90. The figures in the sale contracts conflict with the recollection of Douglas Robinson that sellers were given only $5 on the spot. Robinson was a director of the Stuyvesant Real Estate Company and president of Douglas Robinson, Charles S. Brown Co. Real Estate, the firm originally used by the railroad. For Robinson's description of the acquisition process, see an article on that subject drafted by an assistant, dated August 26, 1910, Hagley Museum and Library, Acc. 1810, Box 149, Folder 7. Rea blocked publication of the article because he wanted the information kept secret.

35. The figure of five hundred houses is given in a souvenir book published by the Pennsylvania Railroad Company, *Pennsylvania Station in New York City* (n. pl., 1910), unpaginated. A smaller number, four hundred houses, is given in "The Excavation for the Pennsylvania Railroad Station, New York," *Scientific American*, XVIV/22 (June 2, 1906), 454. The Pennsylvania Railroad did not release complete data relating to clearance of the station site. Only with regard to the blocks between Ninth and Tenth Avenues, about half of the railyard site, did it specify that ninety-four buildings were demolished; see Pennsylvania Railroad, *Corporate, Financial and Construction History*, 24. A seminar paper by Amanda Johnson aided my understanding of the demolition process.

36. For contracts with house wreckers to demolish buildings on the terminal site, see NYPL, Penn Central Records, Box 91.

37. Relocated to 33rd Street between Ninth and Tenth Avenues, the new Church of St. Michael was built to designs by Napoleon Le Brun & Sons with cut stone salvaged from the demolished buildings. See NYPL, Penn Central Records, Box 90.

38. Unsigned copy of a letter from Alexander Cassatt to the president and board of rapid transit commissioners, May 5, 1902, NYPL, Penn Central Records, Box 91. This payment was only for the two blocks of 32nd Street east of Ninth Avenue. The railroad made another payment of $400,000 in 1906 for the bed of 32nd Street between Ninth and Tenth Avenues. See NYPL, Penn Central Records, Box 90; Pennsylvania Railroad, *Corporate, Financial and Construction History*, 9.

39. In 1899–1900 the Pennsylvania Railroad bought nine hundred acres in Greenville, an area in Jersey City, for an enlarged freight yard, which was built in the following years. On the Greenville freight yard, an integral component of the Pennsylvania's improvement of its New York facilities, see Condit, *Port of New York*, vol. 1, 167–68.

40. Cassatt sent a letter of appointment to McKim later that day. It begins, "Confirming the understanding had at our interview this morning, I beg to say that your firm is appointed architects for the Terminal Station to be erected by the Pennsylvania Railroad Company between Seventh and Eighth Avenues and 31st and 33rd Streets, New York City. . . . The part of the work which will be placed in your charge will be all that above the waiting-room level. The retaining walls up to the street levels and the foundations up to the waiting-room level, and all the work below will be under the charge of the Company's engineers," who were Westinghouse Church Kerr & Co. Letter from Alexander Cassatt to Charles McKim, April 24, 1902, New-York Historical

Society, McKim, Mead & White Corr., Pennsylvania Station (hereafter abbreviated as NYHS, MM&W Corr., Penn Station), File 3.

41. Copies of the telegrams to Mead and Moore are in NYHS, MM&W Corr., Penn Station, File 3. The letter to Burnham is cited by Charles Moore, *The Life and Times of Charles Follen McKim* (Boston, 1929), 274.

42. Telegrams from Charles McKim to Samuel Rea, dated, respectively, May 1, 1902, and April 30, 1902, NYHS, MM&W Corr., Penn Station, File 3.

43. "New York Terminal Situation: Central and Pennsylvania," *Wall Street Journal*, September 4, 1912.

44. Despite extensive documentation about the building process, few original architectural drawings of Pennsylvania Station survive. The only one of the presentation drawings to survive is in Columbia University, Avery Architectural and Fine Arts Library, Dept. of Drawings and Archives (the Museum of the City of New York has glass negatives of the entire set); full-scale specification drawings of signage and various station details by staff architects are in the New-York Historical Society, McKim, Mead & White Collection, Penn Station.

45. Letter from McKim, Mead & White to Louis Dreyer, September 25, 1908. NYHS, MM&W Corr., Penn Station, File 3.

46. Letter from McKim, Mead & White to George Gibbs, October 16, 1908, NYHS, MM&W Corr., Penn Station, File 3.

47. Letter from George Gibbs to unidentified recipient, Sept. 1, 1910, NYHS, MM&W Corr., Penn Station File 3.

48. On the treatment of the plaster and the synthetic stone, see Columbia University, Avery Architectural and Fine Arts Library, Dept. of Drawings and Archives, McKim, Mead & White Collection, Operation Records Notebook, 2.

49. Andrew Dolkart, *Morningside Heights* (New York, 1998), 147.

50. Cited by Leland Roth, *McKim, Mead, & White, Architects* (New York, 1983), 246, from a speech McKim delivered in 1902.

51. Charles Moore, *The Life and Times of Charles Follen McKim* (Boston/New York, 1929), 275.

52. Moore, 303–4.

53. Moore, 275–76.

54. Columbia University, Avery Architectural and Fine Arts Library Library, Dept. of Drawings and Archives, McKim, Mead & White Collection, Operation Records Notebook, 3.

55. William Symmes Richardson published various descriptions of the architectural program of Penn Station. This passage and others below are drawn from an unsigned typescript probably written by Richardson and included in McKim, Mead & White's "Operation Records Notebook" for Penn Station; see Columbia University, Avery Architectural and Fine Arts Library, Dept. of Drawings and Archives, McKim, Mead & White Collection, Operation Records Notebook, 2.

56. "Pennsylvania's New York Station," *Architectural Record* 27 (June 1910), 520.

57. Letter from Rea to Gibbs, October 29, 1910, Hagley Museum and Library, Acc. 1807, Box 148, File 4.

58. Moore, 191–92.

59. Moore, 275.

60. Given McKim's training, his extensive library and his interest in the Roman baths, it seems likely that he saw the reconstruction of the Baths of Caracalla by G. Abel Blouet, *Restaurations des thermes d'Antonin Caracalla* (Paris, 1848), illustrated in Figure 1.56, or the closely related reconstruction by Russian architect S.A. Iwanoff made in 1847–1848 and published later in S.A. Iwanoff and C. Huelsen, *Architektonische Studien. Aus den Thermen des Caracalla*, vol. III, part 2 (Berlin, 1898). On the Baths of Caracalla, see Fikret Yegül, *Baths and Bathing in Classical Antiquity* (New York/Cambridge, Ma., 1992),146–62.

61. Leland M. Roth calculated that the Waiting Hall was 20 percent larger than the frigidarium (which he misidentified as the tepidarium). See Roth, *McKim, Mead & White, Architects* (New York, 1983), 321.

62. Columbia University, Avery Architectural and Fine Arts Library, Dept. of Drawings and Archives, McKim, Mead & White Collection, Operation Records Notebook, 2.

63. Idem.

64. Letter from McKim, Mead & White to George Gibbs, chief engineer of electric traction of the Pennsylvania Railroad, October 7, 1909. NYHS, MM&W Corr. Penn Station, File 3.

65. Cassatt responded indirectly to criticisms of the height of the waiting hall in a letter to McKim: "I thank you very much for the drawing of the Terminal; it looks very attractive. I am quite sure we are going to have a very handsome station, and so far as the elevated construction over the main room is concerned, I pin my faith on you." Letter from Cassatt to McKim, May 1, 1905, NYHS, MM&W Corr., Penn Station, File 3.

66. In order to enhance the light conditions at track level, McKim made the sidewalks extra wide by setting the station back from the building line, by twenty feet on 31st Street and fifteen feet on 33rd Street, and finishing the sidewalks at the standard curb line. The difference in the setbacks relates to the extra width of the LIRR platforms on the 33rd Street side. The side-street setbacks are described in a letter from McKim, Mead & White to George Gibbs, November 11, 1908, Hagley Museum and Library, Acc. 1807, Box 147, Folder 24.

67. Lewis Mumford, *The Brown Decades* (New York, 1931), 59.

68. Unsigned letter, probably by William Symmes Richardson, to George Gibbs, September 28, 1910. Columbia University, Avery Architectural and Fine Arts Library, Dept. of Drawings and Archives, McKim, Mead & White Collection.

69. Idem. George Gibbs incorporated a variant version of this explanation in his article "Station Construction, Road, Track, Yard Equipment, Electric Traction and Locomotives," (Paper 1165 in a special issue on The New York Tunnel Extension of the Pennsylvania Railroad), *Transactions of the American Society of Civil Engineers,* LXIX (October 1910), 251.

70. "The type and scale of lattice work was suggested from the very beginning, as well as the lines and sizes of the arches, noticeably the variation in depth between the spring and top of the lines of the arches, as well as the varying width between the diagonal ribs and main vault lines—thus obtaining a variety of effect and avoiding the monotony which would result in an assemblage of arches of similar form and dimension." Ibid.

71. For a discussion of the structure of the concourse roof, see George B. Francis and Joseph H. O'Brien, "Certain Engineering Structures of the New York Terminal Area" (Paper 1164 in a special issue on The New York Tunnel Extension of the Pennsylvania Railroad), *Transactions of the American Society of Civil Engineers*, LXIX (October 1910), 198.

72. Ibid.

73. Lewis Mumford, "The Disappearance of Pennsylvania Station," *The New Yorker*, June 7, 1958, 107.

74. The ten entrances were located as follows (moving clockwise from the main entrance): Seventh Avenue; 31st Street driveway; 31st Street to waiting room; 31st Street to concourse; Eighth Avenue; 33rd Street to concourse; 33rd Street to stairway to LIRR trains; 33rd Street to waiting hall; 34th Street; and 33rd Street driveway. A survey of the number of people entering and leaving Penn Station made on Saturday, September 1, 1917, indicated that the Seventh Avenue entrance was busiest (39,896 people) followed by the 34th Street entrance (25,492 people). The 31st Street entrance to the waiting hall was the least used (1,846 people). See the memos on passenger traffic from R.V. Massey, General Superintendent of the station, NYPL, Penn Central Records, Box 87.

75. W. Symmes Richardson, "The Terminal—Gate of the City," *Scribner's Magazine* 52/4 (October 1912), 407. George Gibbs claimed credit for inventing the exit concourse as a way of efficiently moving passengers to the subway. He explained the genesis of the idea in a revealing memorandum to Samuel Rea.

The means originally provided to handle passengers from the train platforms to the street was mainly by stairways to the main concourse level and thence by stairs to the rear entrance on Eighth Avenue, the side entrances on 33rd and 31st Streets, or by stairways and ramps through the arcade to Seventh Avenue or up the driveways. When the station was first planned, it was thought that there would undoubtedly be a city subway either on Seventh or Eighth Avenue open about the time the station was completed, and it was felt that the main bulk of passengers who did not take carriages would use the subway and would take the low level passageway under 33rd Street to the subway station. Upon this supposition, you will remember, I brought up to Mr. Cassatt and yourself the advisability of separating the incoming and outgoing passengers at the concourse and suggested that an exit concourse under the main concourse would be desirable.

As the station is now being built, the exit concourse lands passengers on the lower level of the passageway under 33rd Street and at the proper level for them to reach a subway station. It has since become evident that it is hopeless to expect the completion of a subway under Eighth Avenue for some years after our station is opened. This means that the exit concourse will be of very little use, as it lands passengers under 33rd Street with only one stairway directly communicating with the street surface and no other way of exit except by coming up to the main concourse, thus defeating the primary object of the scheme.

The only way, as I see it, of restoring this exit concourse to its usefulness, is by providing an exit from the 33rd Street passageway through property which we own to 34th Street.

This scheme has been discussed many times and I believe you have considered that it would be eventually desirable to provide a private street through our property, but it would seem that in view of the subway situation it is highly desirable to develop plans for this means of exit at once, so that it can be put into operation coincidently with the station.

Letter from Gibbs to Rea, January 5, 1909, Hagley Museum and Library, Acc. 1807, Box 147, Folder 23.

The exit concourse was originally only 60 feet wide, but in the mid-1930s it was extended over the tracks to the west, closing off the spectacular vista from the platforms to the concourse roof.

76. A memo from Gibbs on this subject conveys McKim's historically informed thought process: "It would appear to be best to limit the grade of the inclines to 8 percent, and to accomplish this in the distance we have at our disposal it is necessary to 'step' the inclines, as suggested by Mr. McKim, similar to the method employed in the old Roman structures." Hagley Museum and Library, Acc. 1807, Box 147, Folder 23, "Synopsis of Correspondence from Files of Samuel Rea, #4504," entry dated August 9, 1906.

77. Letter from McKim, Mead & White to Samuel Rea, December 17, 1908, Hagley Museum and Library, Acc. 1807, Box 147, Folder 23. On the connection between the absence of subway outlets and enhancement of the 34th Street entrance, see note 75 above.

78. On demolition of buildings on West 34th Street in December 1909 in order to create the private street, see Hagley Museum and Library, Acc. 1807, Box 147, Folder 23.

79. Letter from George Gibbs to Samuel Rea, April 25, 1910, Hagley Museum and Library, Acc. 1807, Box. 147, Folder 23.

80. Memorandum from George Gibbs to Samuel Rea on "Handling Passengers to and from Station," January 5, 1909, Hagley Museum and Library, Acc. 1807, Box 147, Folder 23.

81. See Richardson, "The Terminal," 406. Gibbs also determined that passengers would have to walk from 1,000 to 1,800 feet to the main arteries of street-car intercommunication.

82. The prevailing practice was to sort and transport luggage on passenger platforms. The system of separate driveways for luggage delivery was pioneered at the turn of the century and introduced at nearly the same time at Union Station in St. Louis, Union Station in Washington, D.C., Grand Central Terminal, and Penn Station. A seminar paper by Elizabeth Rosenberry informed the discussion of luggage handling.

83. For a description of the facilities in the station, including the system of synchronized clocks, see E. J. Bell, "Electric Traction and Station Construction," in William Couper, ed., *History of the Engineering, Construction and Equipment of the Pennsylvania Railroad Company's New York Terminal and Approaches* (New York, 1912), reprinted in Fred Westing, *Penn Station: Its Tunnels and Side Rodders* (Seattle, 1978), 57–70 (hereinafter cited as Couper). For a list of all the clocks and their dimensions, see Hagley Museum and Library, Acc. 1810, Box 146, Folder 5, "Notes on Conferences on New York Terminal Station Facilities, Held Feb. 13, 1908 in New York City and Feb. 25, 1908 at Broad Street Station, Philadelphia."

84. Samuel O. Dunn, "The Problem of the Modern Terminal," *Scribner's Magazine* 52/4 (October 1912), 436.

85. The letter continues: "As a matter of experience, wooden cars operated on an electric line in the open, like the West Jersey & Seashore R.R. and Long Island R.R., would be subject to more causes for fires, although, of course, in the case of the tunnels it would be more disagreeable, but apart from all this other railroads in the country are ordering steel cars for passenger as well as freight business on just the same grounds that we are, namely, a realization that it is the best car for modern railroad conditions." Letter from Samuel Rea to W. W. Atterbury, general manager, and J. R. Wood, passenger traffic manager, March 2, 1909, Hagley Museum and Library, Acc. 1810, Box 149, Folder 21.

86. The Pennsylvania Railroad sold the power plant at Hunter's Point to Consolidated Edison in 1938. For further information about the two generating stations, see Couper, *History of the Engineering, Construction and Equipment*, 69, 74.

87. Leland M. Roth, *McKim, Mead & White, Architects* (New York, 1983), cited on 317.

88. Letter from Gustav Lindenthal to Samuel Rea, December 21, 1910, Hagley Museum and Library, Acc. 1807, Box 141, Folder 5.

89. Letter from Samuel Rea to the Pennsylvania Railroad's Committee on New York Real Estate, March 8, 1912, Hagley Museum and Library, Acc. 1807, Box 148, Folder 2.

90. Letter from Samuel Rea to Bert Hanson, December 6, 1910, Hagley Museum and Library, Acc. 1810, Box 141, Folder 5.

91. Once the railroad resolved to make the 34th Street entrance into a private street, Rea supported a northern extension from 34th to 42nd Street; see his letters to Douglas Robinson, April 3, 1909, and to George McAneny, Manhattan Borough president, January 13, 1910, Hagley Museum and Library Acc. 1807, Box 147, Folder 23.

92. The diagonal boulevard was proposed in 1911 by architect Henry Rutgers Marshall, who did not wish to publicize the Pennsylvania Railroad's support for a telling reason. "Inasumuch as the city had entirely disregarded the wishes of the Pennsylvania officials in regard to the subway matter, there might be a danger of their dealing with the proposed Avenue in the same way." Letter from E. R. Hill, assistant to the chief engineer to Samuel Rea, November 14, 1911, Hagley Museum and Library, Acc. 1807, Box 141, Folder 15. This file contains correspondence, newspaper articles, and other materials relating to the diagonal boulevard.

93. On distances from Penn Station to the various forms of public transportation in the area, see Gibbs's memorandum on passenger traffic, Hagley Museum and Library, Acc. 1807, Box 147, Folder 23.

94. Letter from Augustus H. Ivins to Samuel Rea, December 13, 1912, Hagley Museum and Library, Acc. 1807, Box 148, Folder 3.

95. For the terms of the air-rights conveyance for the Post Office site, see NYPL, Penn Central Records, Box 13, Minutebook of the Pennsylvania, New York and Long Island Railroad Company, June 7, 1906, 232. The contract required the Pennsylvania Railroad to build an underground passageway between the post office and the Seventh Avenue subway, if such a line were built. For Rea's interest in the building's design, see his letter to William R. Mead, January 25, 1908, and Mead's reply, January 27, 1908, NYHS, MM&W 1950 Coll., N.Y. Post Office Main Building,

Box 14-14c, File 14c. For documentation concerning the architectural competition, McKim, Mead & White's design, and the mail handling equipment, see NYHS, MM&W 1950 Coll., N.Y. Post Office Main Building, Boxes 14-1 to 14-1f, 14-14c (see file 14a for statistics on the volume of mail and mail trains to be handled at the new post office), 14-13a to 14-32c, 14-2 to 14-12c. For William Kendall's consultation with various scholars to compose the famous inscription based on Herodotus, see NYHS, MM&W Corr., Mixed File 509; and NYPL, Penn Central Records, Box 92.

96. On Rea's interest in air-rights development of the railyard, see his memo to Benjamin Carskaddon, real estate agent of the Pennsylvania Railroad, May 27, 1907, Hagley Museum and Library, Acc. 1807, Box 148, Folder 7; and letter from Samuel Rea to Henry C. Frick, October 7, 1908, Hagley Museum and Library, Acc. 1807, Box 145, Folder 20.

97. On Gibbs's objections to air-rights development, see his letter to Rea, May 5, 1909, Hagley Museum and Library, Acc. 1807, Box 145, Folder 20. Almost immediately after the Post Office opened in 1913, it was deemed necessary to build an expansion, but the acquisition process was protracted. In 1931 the railroad conveyed the air rights to the west half of the block between Eighth and Ninth Avenues, 31st and 33rd Streets, to the U.S. government, subject to an easement for operation of the railroad. For documentation concerning the Post Office Annex, see the archival references in note 95.

98. In McKim's original proposal the station was set back 24 feet from the building line. It was subsequently moved closer to Seventh Avenue in order to make easier gradients for the driveway. The curb was set back 7½ feet from the standard line. Letter from Samuel Rea to H. C. Frick, a member of the railroad's Special Committee on New York Real Estate, October 7, 1908, Hagley Museum and Library, Acc. 1810, Box 149, Folder 7.

99. Letter from Samuel Rea to H. C. Frick, October 7, 1908; letter from Samuel Rea to John McCrea, October 13, 1908, Hagley Museum and Library Acc. 1810, Box 149, Folder 7.

100. Letter from William R. Mead to William Symmes Richardson, May 25, 1912, NYPL, Penn Central Records, Box 82.

101. The Gimbel brothers had their architect, E. R. Graham of D. H. Burnham & Company, negotiate with the Pennsylvania Railroad; see Hagley Museum and Library, Acc. 1807, Box 147, File 24.

102. Letter from Samuel Rea to John McCrea, September 13, 1908, Hagley Museum and Library, Acc. 1807, Box 145, File 20.

103. Letter from Samuel Rea to Walter Oakman, president of the Hudson Companies, May 5, 1908, Hagley Museum and Library, Acc. 1807, Box 145, File 20.

104. Letter from Samuel Rea to Gustav Lindenthal, April 6, 1911, Hagley Museum and Library, Acc. 1807, Box 148, File 2. Eleven parcels in Manhattan were recommended for sale, most of them small lots that had been acquired for building tunnel shafts during construction of the cross-town tunnels. See the report of the Special Committee on New York Real Estate, December 30, 1910, Hagley Museum and Library, Acc. 1807, Box 148, File 1.

105. Letter from Benjamin Carskaddon, real estate agent, to James McCrea, president of the Pennsylvania Railroad, June 12, 1911, Hagley Museum and Library, Acc. 1807, Box 148, Folder 1.

106. On discussions with Gimbel Brothers, see Hagley Museum and Library, Acc. 1807, Box

145, Folder 20. For a prospectus of a mercantile building and correspondence concerning possible connections through the store to transit facilities on Seventh and Sixth Avenues, see Hagley Museum and Library, Acc. 1807, Box 147, Folder 24, and Box 148, Folder 2. On the purchase of the 32nd Street property, known as the Dimond property, see Hagley Museum and Library, Acc. 1807, Box 148, Folder 2.

107. Although Gimbel Brothers said they were unable to raise the $3 million needed to stock and furnish the proposed addition to their store, the railroad understood that they had the means but not the desire to do so. See the memorandum from A. J. County to Samuel Rea, Hagley Museum and Library, Acc. 1807, Box 148, Folder 3.

108. *New York Sun,* August 25, 1912.

109. Letter from Augustus H. Ivins to Samuel Rea, December 13, 1912, Hagley Museum and Library, Acc. 1807, Box 148, Folder 3.

110. Letter from Wm. Sittenham to the president and board of directors of the Pennsylvania Railroad, September 18, 1912, Hagley Museum and Library, Acc. 1807, Box 148, Folder 3.

111. Letter from Samuel Rea to C. S. Mellen, June 16, 1913, NYPL, Penn Central Records, Box 87.

112. "New York Terminal Situation; New York Central and Pennsylvania," *Wall Street Journal,* September 4, 1912.

113. Ibid.

114. On the hotel scheme, see the letter from Samuel Rea to B. W. Carskaddon, January 17, 1907, Hagley Museum and Library, Acc. 1807, Box 147, Folder 23. The shop scheme is discussed in "Tides of Traffic about Pennsylvania Terminal," *The Globe,* March 9, 1910. On the proposed apartment buildings on 31st Street, see Hagley Museum and Library, Box 147, Folder 23.

115. Letter from Ernst Todd, Seaboard Realty Co., to Frank Widner Jr., Alvan Perry Real Estate and Mortgage Investments, Hagley Museum and Library, Acc. 1807, Box 148, Folder 1.

116. See the inventory of hotel proposals prepared by Benjamin Carskaddon, November 29, 1912, Hagley Museum and Library, Acc. 1807, Box 148, Folder 3. The Pennsylvania Terminal Real Estate Company was incorporated on October 28, 1912. Railroad properties previously held by the Stuyvesant Real Estate Company and the Pennsylvania Tunnel and Terminal Railroad Company were transferred to the new corporation.

117. Letter from Samuel Rea to R. Beinecke, president of the Plaza Operating Co., July 11, 1908, Hagley Museum and Library, Acc. 1807, Box 145, Folder 20.

118. In 1948 the Pennsylvania Railroad sold the hotel and underlying land, with an easement for railroad operations at track level, to the Hotel Statler. On construction and financing of the Hotel Pennsylvania, see NYPL, Penn Central Records, Box 81.

119. The Pennsylvania Railroad's files contain detailed comparative information about the two hotels; see NYPL, Penn Central Records, Box 82.

120. On construction of the underground passage, see NYPL, Penn Central Records, Box 85.

121. Cited by Alfred D. Chandler, Jr., *The Visible Hand. The Managerial Revolution in American Business* (Cambridge, Mass./London, 1977), 176.

122. Condit, *Port of New York,* vol. 1, 392, note 59; vol. 2, 163, 277–78.

123. The data and quotation are cited by Stephen Salsbury, *No Way to Run a Railroad: The Untold Story of the Penn Central Crisis* (New York, 1982), 30–31.

124. Statistics come from Kenneth Smith, "Competition and Costs. As Business Drops, Railroads Turn to Mergers to Reduce Expenses," *New York Times,* January 13, 1962, 8.

125. The data comes from Robert Sobel, *The Fallen Colossus* (New York, 1977), 222–23.

126. Salsbury, *No Way to Run a Railroad,* 32.

127. Sobel, *Fallen Colossus,* 230.

128. Joseph R. Daughen and Peter Binzen, *The Wreck of the Penn Central* (Boston, 1971), 312–13.

129. Memo from W.R.G. to David Bevan, vice-president for finance, September 24, 1952, Hagley Museum and Library, Acc. 1810, Box 257, Folder 11.

130. "Site of Proposed Garage Atop Penn Station," *New York Herald Tribune,* September 13, 1950, 15.

131. Memorandum from P.D.F. to David Bevan, vice-president for finance, September 18, 1952, Hagley Museum and Library, Acc. 1810, Box 257, Folder 11. Other documents relating to the 1952 proposal are in the same box.

132. For documents relating to the air rights west of Ninth Avenue, see Hagley Museum and Library, Acc. 1810, Box 257, Folder 11.

133. Peter Kihss, " 'Palace' is Slated For Penn Station," *New York Times,* June 8, 1955, 1:4.

134. "Using City Air Space That's Valuable," June 16, 1955, article clipped from unidentified magazine in the office files of McKim, Mead & White, NYHS, MM&W Corr., Penn Station, File 981.

135. On negotiations with Zeckendorf and internal railroad analyses of the proposal, see Hagley Museum and Library, Acc. 1810, Box 257, Folder 11.

136. Editorial, "A New 'Penn Depot,' " *New York Times,* June 4, 1955, 14:3. See also another editorial, "Palace of Progress," *New York Times,* June 9, 1955, 28:3.

137. John C. Devlin, "Zeckendorf Maps New Penn Station," *New York Times,* November 30, 1954, 1:5. See also the follow-up stories, "New Penn Station Set in Big Project," *New York Times,* June 4, 1955, 1:3; Peter Kihss, " 'Palace' is Slated for Penn Station," *New York Times,* June 8, 1955, 1:4.

138. Notes of Lawrence Grant White, October 19, 1954, NYHS, MM&W Corr., File 981.

139. Letter from James Symes to William Zeckendorf, July 11, 1956, Hagley Museum and Library, Acc. 1810, Box 257, Folder 11.

140. Symes stated, "If the structure were leveled and turned into a parking lot, not only would the Pennsylvania save money, but it might more readily find a tenant for the land." Robert Bedingfield, "Pennsy Expects Only a Fair Year," *New York Times,* May 11, 1960, 57.

141. "Penn Station — New York, Proposed Redevelopment Preliminary Report, 3-23-60," Hagley Museum and Library, Acc. 1810, Box 257, Folder 12.

142. "Topics," *New York Times,* September 10, 1960, 20:3.

143. Robert Bedingfield, "Merger of Pennsylvania and New York Central Is Approved by Directors," *New York Times,* January 13, 1962, 1:8.

144. On Penn Center, see Salsbury, *No Way to Run a Railroad,* 58; "Pennsy Sells Air Rights In Philadelphia Area," *New York Times,* December 7, 1960, 75:2.

145. The plan for a 40-story tower is disclosed in "Concerns Plan $75 Million Entertainment Center Over New York's Penn Station," *Wall Street Journal,* July 27, 1961, 5:1.

146. The schedule of payments was complex: $400,000 for the first 16 months; $675,000 for the following year; $1 million annually from 1965 to 1988. Thereafter the railroad was guaranteed a minimum of $1,050,000 per year. The lease was presumably annulled when the Penn Central declared bankruptcy. Thanks to Christopher Baer, who located the lease for me in Hagley Museum and Library, Acc. 1810, Box 257. Also see "Raising a New Garden," *BusinessWeek,* February 23, 1963, 142.

147. "Concerns Plan $75 Million Entertainment Center Over New York's Penn Station," *Wall Street Journal,* July 27, 1961, 5:1.

148. In 1968 the railroad's stock in the Madison Square Garden Center had a market value of $25.7 million. A reorganization took place in 1968 when the Penn Central was formed. Penn Central exchanged its holdings for a 23 percent interest in a Madison Square Garden Corporation, which was reorganized as a holding company for various entities, including two professional sports teams, the New York Knickerbockers and the New York Rangers. The Penn Central subsequently bought additional stock and expanded its interest to 24 percent. See Salsbury, *No Way to Run a Railroad,* 58–59; Daughen and Binzen, *Wreck of the Penn Central,* 244–47.

149. Changing plans for the Madison Square Garden Center can be tracked in newspaper accounts between July 1961 and 1964, when the plans were finalized.

150. "Pennsy Official Says Merging U.S. Rails Into Big Systems Might Solve Money Woes," *Wall Street Journal,* March 24, 1961, 6:3.

151. "Pennsy Executive Sees Merger Savings Delay," *New York Times,* November 7, 1962, 61:5; "Pennsy and N.Y. Central Outline Expected Savings from Merger," *New York Times,* November 12, 1962, 47:2.

152. Salsbury, *No Way to Run a Railroad,* 135.

153. Foster Hailey, "Battle over the Future of Penn Station Continues," *New York Times,* September 23, 1962, 78:1.

154. Advertisement, "Save Our City," *New York Times,* August 2, 1962, 14:7.

155. Editorial, "Saving Fine Architecture," *New York Times,* August 11, 1962, 16:1.

156. Letter to the editor from A. J. Greenough, "Redeveloping Penn Station," *New York Times,* August 23, 1962, 28:6.

157. Foster Hailey, "Battle over the Future of Penn Station Continues," *New York Times,* September 23, 1962, 78:1.

158. Letter to the editor from Norval White, *New York Times,* May 17, 1962, 36:6.

159. Ibid. The proposal was endorsed and promoted by AGBANY.

160. The legislation was enacted on May 10, 1962. Jameson Doig, *Metropolitan Transportation Politics and the New York Region* (New York, 1966), 30, 218–20.

161. "Felt Gives View on Penn Station," *New York Times,* August 26, 1962, 70:4. One of the votes for the variance came from Harmon Goldstone, who served on both the City Planning Commission and the Committee for the Preservation of Structures of Historic and Aesthetic

Importance. Goldstone was chairman of the Landmarks Preservation Commission from 1968 to 1973. On Goldstone, see Christopher Gray, "On Preservation, 'I Told You So,'" *New York Times,* July 12, 1992, Section 10, 7:1; and David Dunlap, "Harmon Goldstone Dies at 89," *New York Times,* February 23, 2001, A17:1.

162. Condit, *Port of New York,* vol. 2, 253.

163. "Farewell to Penn Station, *New York Times,* October 30, 1963.

164. The leaders of the Pennsylvania Station Redevelopment Corporation have discovered other ruins still buried in the Meadowlands. The future of these pieces remains uncertain.

165. See Barbara Moore, ed., *The Destruction of Penn Station: Photographs by Peter Moore* (New York, 2000). Aaron Rose has donated his demolition photographs to the Museum of the City of New York. The New-York Historical Society has a series of demolition photographs by Al Hatos, a life-long employee of the Pennsylvania Railroad, covering the period from March 1964 to June 1967. One virtue of this series is that every image is dated.

166. Statement by Max Silverman, January 1980, uncataloged document, Museum of the City of New York.

167. My summary draws on the following sources in addition to the coverage in the *New York Times:* Eric Allison, "Historic Preservation in a Development-Dominated City: The Passage of New York City's Landmark Preservation Legislation," *Journal of Urban History* 22/3 (March 1996), 350–76; Harmon Goldstone and Martha Dalrymple, *History Preserved. A Guide to New York City Landmarks and Historic Districts* (New York, 1974); and Anthony Wood, "Pioneers of Preservation," *Village Views,* vol. 4, no. 1 (Winter 1987), no. 3 (Summer 1987), and no. 4 (Fall 1987).

168. Allison, "Historic Preservation," 355.

169. Charles Bennett, "City Acts to Save Historical Sites," *New York Times,* April 22, 1962, 1:4.

170. On the role of James Felt, see Allison, "Historic Preservation," 357–58, 364–69; and Goldstone and Dalrymple, *History Preserved,* 19–20.

171. On historic buildings demolished in the early 1960s, see Ada Louise Huxtable, "To Keep the Best of New York," *New York Times,* September 10, 1961, Section 6, 44; Huxtable, "Worth Street Losing Its Historic Aura," *New York Times,* December 1, 1962, 27:2; and Huxtable, "Goodbye Worth Street: A New York Tragedy," *New York Times,* December 2, 1962, Section 2, 17:5; Thomas Ennis, "Landmark Mansion on 79th St. to be Razed," *New York Times,* September 17, 1964, 1:2. Demolition of the Brokaw houses was carried out in February 1965. The Percy Pyne Mansion was saved; see below in text.

172. Editorial, "Landmark Legislation," *New York Times,* December 3, 1964, 44:1. Also see the lead editorial, "Anything Left to Preserve?" on September 24, 1964: "This is a city being ruthlessly rebuilt—a process in which progress has merely become a misspelling of profit—at the near-total sacrifice of its distinctive urban quality." *New York Times,* September 24, 1964, 40:1.

173. On the hearings and final vote, see "City Holds Landmarks Bill Hearing," *New York Times,* December 4, 1964, 53:6; "Bill on Landmarks Approved by Council," *New York Times,* April 7, 1965, 87:4; Thomas Ennis, "Landmarks Get City Protection," *New York Times,* April 11, 1965, Section 8, 1:8.

174. Cited by Allison, "Historic Preservation," 373.

175. Charles V. Bagli, "Cablevision Considers Rebuilding Madison Square Garden," *New York Times,* March 21, 2000, B3.

Select Bibliography

Belle, John, and Leighton, Maxinne R. *Grand Central: Gateway to a Million Lives*. New York: W. W. Norton, 2000.

Bezilla, Michael. *Electric Traction on the Pennsylvania Railroad, 1895–1968*. University Park, Penn.: Pennsylvania State University Press, 1980.

Condit, Carl. *The Port of New York: A History of the Rail and Terminal System from the Beginnings to Pennsylvania Station*. Chicago/London: The University of Chicago Press, 1980.

———. *The Port of New York: A History of the Rail and Terminal System from the Grand Central Electrification to the Present*. Chicago/London: The University of Chicago, 1981.

Couper, William, ed. *History of the Engineering, Construction and Equipment of the Pennsylvania Railroad Company's New York Terminal and Approaches*. New York: Isaac H. Blanchard Company, 1912. Reprinted in Fred Westing, *Penn Station: Its Tunnels and Side Rodders*. Seattle: Superior Publishing Company, 1978.

Cudahy, Brian J. *Under the Sidewalks of New York. The Story of the Greatest Subway System in the World*, 2nd rev. ed. New York: Fordham University Press, 1995.

Daughen, Joseph R., and Binzen, Peter. *The Wreck of the Penn Central*. Boston: Little, Brown, 1971.

Davis, Patricia T. *End of the Line. Alexander J. Cassatt and the Pennsylvania Railroad*. New York: Neale Watson Academic Publications, 1978.

Derrick, Peter. *Tunneling to the Future. The Story of the Great Subway Expansion that Saved New York*. New York: New York University Press, 2001.

Diehl, Lorraine B. *The Late, Great Pennsylvania Station*, 2nd ed. New York/London: Four Walls, Eight Windows, 1985.

Droege, John A. *Passenger Terminals and Trains*. New York: McGraw Hill, 1916. Reprint ed. Milwaukee, Wisc.: Kalmbach, 1969.

Dunn, Samuel O. "The Problem of the Modern Terminal," *Scribner's Magazine*, LII/4 (October 1912), 416–42.

Meeks, Carroll L. V. *The Railroad Station. An Architectural History*, 2nd ed. Mineola, New York: Dover Publications, 1995.

Middleton, William D. *Manhattan Gateway. New York's Pennsylvania Station*. Waukesha, Wisc.: Kalmbach, 1996.

Moore, Barbara, ed. *The Destruction of Penn Station: Photographs by Peter Moore*. New York: D.A.P., 2000.

Moore, Charles. *The Life and Times of Charles Follen McKim*. Boston/New York: Houghton Mifflin, 1929.

"The New York Tunnel Extension of the Pennsylvania Railroad," Papers 1150–1165, *Transactions of the American Society of Civil Engineers* 68 (January 1910), and 69 (October 1910).

Parissien, Steven. *Pennsylvania Station. McKim, Mead and White*. London: Phaidon, 1996.

The Pennsylvania Railroad Company. Corporate, Financial and Construction History of Lines Owned, Operated and Controlled to December 31, 1945, vol. 2, Lines East of Pittsburgh. New York: Coverdale & Colpitts Consulting Engineers, 1946.

[Pennsylvania Railroad Company]. *The New York Improvement and Tunnel Extension of the Pennsylvania Railroad*. Philadelphia: Pennsylvania Railroad Company, 1910.

Powell, Kenneth. *Grand Central Terminal. Warren and Wetmore*. London: Phaidon, 1996.

Richardson, W. Symmes. "The Terminal — The Gate of the City," *Scribner's Magazine*, LII/4 (October 1912), 401–16.

Roth, Leland. *McKim, Mead & White, Architects*. New York: Harper & Row, 1983.

Roth, Leland. "The Urban Architecture of McKim, Mead & White: 1870–1910," 2 vols. Ph.D. dissertation. Yale University, 1973.

Salsbury, Stephen. *No Way to Run a Railroad. The Untold Story of the Penn Central Crisis*. New York: McGraw-Hill, 1982.

Schlichting, Kurt C. *Grand Central Terminal. Railroads, Engineering, and Architecture in New York City*. Baltimore/London: The Johns Hopkins University Press, 2001.

Schotter, H[oward]. W[ard]. *The Growth and Development of the Pennsylvania Railroad Company. A Review of the Charter and Annual Reports of the Pennsylvania Railroad Company 1846 to 1926, Inclusive*. Philadelphia: Allen, Lane & Scott, 1927.

Sobel, Robert. *The Fallen Colossus*. New York: Weybright and Talley, 1977.

Stern, Robert A. M., Gilmartin, Gregory, and Massengale, John. *New York 1900. Metropolitan Architecture and Urbanism 1890–1915*. New York: Rizzoli, 1983.

Stilgoe, John R. *Metropolitan Corridor. Railroads and the American Scene*. New Haven/London: Yale University Press, 1983.

Westinghouse Church Kerr & Company Engineers. *The New York Passenger Terminal and Improvement of the Pennsylvania and Long Island Railroads Relating to the Work Performed by Westinghouse Church Kerr & Co. Engineers*. New York, 1910.

Photography Credits

Arif Turkeli: Figs. 1.1–1.3; 1.79.

Avery Architectural and Fine Arts Library, Columbia University: 1.4; 1.20; 1.22–1.38; 1.40;
 1.43; 1.45–1.46; 1.49; 1.51–1.64; 1.67; 1.69–1.71; 1.73; 1.78.

Hilary Ballon: 1.44.

Brown Brothers: 1.19; 1.39; 1.41.

Jock Pottle/Esto: Figs. 3.9; 3.19.

Farley Post Office Archives: 3.26.

Hagley Museum and Library: 1.8; 1.9; 1.74; 1.80-81.

Long Island University, Heller Collection of Transit and Construction Photographs: 1.5-7;
 1.10-13; 1.15-17.

Chris Lovi: Figs. 3.5; 3.30–3.31.

Norman McGrath: Page 15; 1.42; 2.1–2.49, 3.5; 3.31.

Museum of the City of New York, Byron Collection: 1.14.

New-York Historical Society: 1.18; 1.21; 1.47; 1.48; 1.50; 1.65; 1.66; 1.68; 1.72; 1.75–1.77.

pixelbypixel with SOM: 3.1; 3.20; 3.27; 3.28; 3.32

Skidmore Owings & Merrill: 3.2–3.4; 3.6–3.8; 3.10–3.18; 3.21–3.25; 3.33–3.36.

Ron Ziel: 1.82.

Index

Page numbers in italics refer to selected figures in the text.

Action Group for Better Architecture in
   New York (AGBANY), 101, 102
American Museum of Natural History, 56
Americas Society, 103
Amtrak, 101, 157, 158, 159, 160, *170*, *172*, 174, 175
Ancient Rome, 12, 19, 41, 52, 55, 56, 61, 65, 66,
   69, 104
Architectural League, 82
Architectural Record, 36, 56, 64
Army Corps of Engineers, 23
Arup and Parsons Brinckerhoff, 159
Avedon, Richard, 112

Baldwin, William, 35
Baltimore & Ohio Railroad, 22
Baltimore, Md., 21
Bank of England, London, England, 59
Basilica of Constantine, 66
Baths of Caracalla, 65, 66, 166
Baths of Diocletian, 66
Baths of Titus, 66
Bergen Hill, N.J., 24
Bergen Hill Tunnels, *26*, *27*, *28*

Bernini, Gianlorenzo, 59
Bevan, David, 98, 99
Board of Rapid Transit Commissioners, 38
Boston, Mass., 105, 157, 192
Boston Public Library, 54, 58
Brandenburg Gate, Berlin, Germany, 59
Brennan, William, 107
Breuer, Marcel, 107
Brodovitch, Alexey, 112, 115
Brokaw houses, 106
Bronx, New York City, N.Y., 22, 25
Brooklyn Bridge, 19, 23
Brooklyn Museum, 41, 104
Brooklyn, New York City, N.Y., 22, 24, 92
Burnham, Daniel H., 41, 56, 65, 76

Campidoglio, Rome, Italy, 75
Canadian Centre for Architecture, 163, 190
Cantor, H. B., 95
Carnegie Hall, 103
Cassatt, Alexander, 24, 25, 40, 41, 43, 65, 78,
   79, 87, 94
Charleston, S.C., 105

Chicago, Ill., 20, 21, 99, 100

City and South London Railway, London, England, 22

City Hall (New York City), 17, 64

City Planning Commission (New York City), 95, 103, 106

Clinton, Bill, 162

Cologne train station, Germany, *66*

Columbia University, 41, 54; Low Library, 50, 52; School of Architecture, 19, 52

Committee for the Preservation of Structures of Historic and Aesthetic Importance, 105

Committee of Fifteen, 35

Con Agg Recycling Corporation, 104

Condit, Carl, 11

Cooper Union for the Advancement of Science and Art, 102

Corbitt, Harvey Wiley, 74

Creighton, Thomas, 102

Crow, Jules, 43, 73, 82, *86*

Cuevas, Marquesa de, 103

Diehl, Lorraine, 11

Dreyer, Louis H., 12, 43, 46, 50

Eagle Scout Tribute Fountain, Kansas City, Mo., 104

East River (New York City), 18, 19, 22, 24, 25, 78, 155

Ecole des Beaux-Arts (Paris), 65

Eisenman, Peter, 191, *192*

Elevated rail lines, 33, *36*, *38*, 76, *85*

Empire State Building, 112, *130*

Empire State Development Corporation (ESDC), 159, 160

Farley (James A.) Building, *See* United States General Post Office

Federal Railroad Administration (FRA), 159, 160

Felt, Irving Mitchell, 99, 100, 102, 106

Felt, James, 106

Ferries, 19, 20, 22

Ferriss, Hugh, 74

Flagg, Ernest, 74

Flatiron Building, 54

Forbes, Will, 111

FRA, *See* Federal Railroad Administration

Frankfurt train station, Germany, 69

Freeman, Mark, 104

Frick, Henry, 86

Fuller (George A.) Construction Company, 51

Gare de l'Est, Paris, France, 67

Gare d'Orsay, Paris, France, 24

Gateway Center, Chicago, Ill., 100

General Services Administration (GSA), 159

Generating station, *See* Power house

George Washington Bridge, 102

Gibbs, George, 51, 64, 76, 86

Gimbel Brothers Department Store, 87, 88, 89, 91

Giurgola, Romaldo, 101

Goldstone, Harmon, 106

Graham-Paige (investment house), 99

Grand Army Plaza, 41

Grand Central Terminal, 12, 24, 33, 56, *57*, 58, 76, 78, 79, 80, 81, 82, 83, 89, 90, 91, 93, 107, 157, 158, 181

Greeley Square, 33

Greenough, A. J., 102

Greenville, N.J., 38

Greyhound bus terminal, 90

Guerin, Jules, 66

Hackensack Meadowlands, N.J., 24

Hackensack, N.J., *26*, *27*

Hardy Holzman Pfeiffer, 159

Harper's Bazaar, 112

Harrison, N.J., 24

Haskin, DeWitt Clinton, 22

Hell Gate, 22, 36

Hell Gate Bridge, 23, 25

Hell's Kitchen, 162

Herald Square, 33, 82, 83, 89

Herald Tribune, 96

Herodotus, 165

Historic landmarks, 103, 105–107, 159, 160, 161, 175, 176, 184, 185, 186, 187

Historic preservation, 101–103, 105–107, 160

Hotel Biltmore, 91

Hotel Governor Clinton, 95

Hotel Pennsylvania, *45*, 91, 111, 113, *130*, *133*, *149*

Hotel Statler, 91

Hudson and Manhattan Railroad Company, 33, 87, 89, 92, 102

Hudson Companies, 87, 88, 89

Hudson River, 18, 19, 20, 21, 22, 23, 24, 27, 33, 36, 43, 155, 162, 191

Hudson River Tunnels, 27, *28*, *29*, 34

Hudson Terminal Buildings, 17, 42, 92

Hunter's Point, Queens, New York City, N.Y., 78

Huxtable, Ada Louise, 101

Idlewild (New York International Airport), *See* Kennedy (John F.) International Airport

Interstate Commerce Commission, 94, 100

IRT (Interborough Rapid Transit Subway), 33, 76, 83

Javits (Jacob K.) Convention Center, 162, 163

Jersey City, N.J., 19, 20, 21, 22, 36, 64

J.F.K. International Airport, *See* Kennedy (John F.) International Airport

JFKJAT, 160

Johnson, Philip, 101

Joint Management Committee, 159

Keavney, Francis, 111

Kendall, William, 164

Kennedy (John F.) International Airport, 102, 154–155, 157, 158, 160, 192, *193*

LaGuardia Airport, 102, 154–155, 158, 191

Lambert, Phyllis, 163, 190

Landmarks Preservation Commission, 105–106, 107, 189

Late, Great Pennsylvania Station, 11

LCOR, 159, 160

L'Enfant, Pierre, 41

Lindenthal, Gustav, 22–23, 25, 79

LIRR, *See* Long Island Railroad

Long Island City, Queens, New York City, N.Y., 22, 24

Long Island Railroad (LIRR), 22, 24, 35, 64, 66, 78, 92, 93, 94, 101, 157, 158, 167, 174

Louisiana Purchase Exposition (St. Louis, Mo., 1904), 43, 82

Luckman, Charles, 104

Machette, Franklin J., 91

Macy (R. H.) & Company, 33, *53*

Madison Square Garden, 99, 100, 103, 104, 105, 107, *136*, *139*, *148*, *149*, *155*, *157*, 162, 191

Madison Square Presbyterian Church, 35

Madison Square Tower, 54

Manhattan Bridge, 22

Manhattan, New York City, N.Y., 18, 19, 21, 22, 23, 24, 27, 33, 35, 38, 40, 41, 54, 74, 78, 83, 86, 90, 92, 95, 104, 155, 162, 163, 190

Manhattan Transfer, 24, 25

Manhattan Tunnels, *30*, *31*, *32*

McCrea, James, 87, 88

McGrath, Norman, 104, 105, *115*

McKim, Charles Follen, 11, 12, 40, 41, 42, 43, 50, 52, 53, 54, 55, 56, 58, 59, 61, 62, 64, 65, 66, 67, 69, 70, 71, 73, 74, 75, 76, 77, 79, 80, 81, 83, 85, 86, 87, 93, 96, 99, 104, 105, *177*, *182*

McKim, Mead & White, 12, 41, 43, 50, 52, 55, 66, 70, 75, 78, 79, 85, 87, 91, 97, 156, 164, 167, 181, 184

Mead, William Rutherford, 40, 87

Metropolitan Commuter Transportation Authority, 101

Metropolitan Life Insurance Building, 54

Metropolitan Museum of Art, 56

Metropolitan Transportation Authority, New York City Transit, 163

Milford, Mass., 51

Moore, Charles, 40, 59, 65

Moore, Peter, 104

Moynihan, Daniel Patrick, 158, 162

Mumford, Lewis, 69, 74

Municipal Art Society, 82, 105

Museum of the City of New York, 114

New England, 22, 24, 25

New Haven line, *See* New York, New Haven and Hartford Railroad

New Jersey, 18, 155, 163

New Jersey Transit (NJT), 157, 158, 174

New Orleans, La., 105

New York 2012 Olympics Committee, 163

New York Central Railroad Company, 20, 78, 79, 81, 86, 89, 90, 100, 107

New York City Landmarks Commission, *See* Landmarks Preservation Commission

New York City, N.Y., 18, 19, 21, 22, 33, 41, 54, 56, 76, 79, 81, 82, 86, 89, 94, 99, 100, 101, 103, 105, 107, 111, 153, 157, 159, 160, 161, 176, 191, 192, 196

New York City Railway Company, 76

New York City subway system, *See* Subway system (New York City)

New York Community Trust, 105

New York Connecting Railroad, 25, 33

New York Daily News, 104

New York extension, Pennsylvania Railroad,

23, 24, 25, 35, 78, 82, 92; *See also* New York Connecting Railroad

New York Herald, 35

New York, New Haven and Hartford Railroad, 22, 25

New York, New Haven and Hudson River Railroad Company, 89

New York Public Library, 56

New York Sun, 89

New York Times, 96, 97, 98, 101, 102, 104, 106, 161

Newark International Airport, 102, 154–155, 157, 158, 191, *193*

Newark, N.J., 92

Newman, William H., 79

NJT, *See* New Jersey Transit

Noble, Alfred, 25

Norfolk & Western Railroad, 93, 94

North River Bridge (unbuilt), 23

North River Tunnels, *See* Hudson River Tunnels

Olmsted, Frederick Law, Jr., 65

One Penn Plaza, 100

O'Rourke Engineering Construction Company, 27

Oud, J. J. P., 101

Panama Canal, 25

Parkhurst, Rev. Charles, 35

PATH (Port Authority Trans-Hudson) Corporation, 17, 33, 102, 163, 167

Penn Center, Philadelphia, Pa., 100

Penn Central Transportation Co. vs. the City of New York, 107

Pennsylvania Railroad Company, 12, 17, 18, 19, 20, 21, 23, 24, 25, 26, 33, 35, 37, 40, 41, 42, 43, 66, 74, 77, 78, 79, 81, 82, 83, 85, 86, 87, 88, 89, 90, 91, 92, 93, 95, 96, 97, 98, 99, 100, 101, 102, 105; merger with New York

Central Railroad Company (Penn Central), 100, 107

Pennsylvania Station Development Corporation, 11

Pennsylvania Station (First), 12, 17–107, 111–115, *116–149*, 153, 158, 185

    clocks, 54, 58, 77, 103, 104

    and commerce, 18, 21, 33, 73

    commercial arcade, 60, 62, *63*, 73, 77, *128, 129, 132*

    and commuters, 92–93

    concourse, 18, *47, 48, 49*, 50, *60*, 61, 67–73, 74, 76, 104, *116, 132, 133, 134, 135, 136, 137, 138, 139*, 181

    construction, 38, *39*, 40, 43, *44, 45*, 46, *47, 48, 49, 50*, 51, 52

    Day and Night (sculpture), 58, 104

    demolition, 19, 52, 95, 96, 97, 99, 101–105, 106, 111–115, *116–149*, 162

    design, 42, 43, 53–55, 56, 58, 59, 60, 69

    eagles (sculptures), 58, 104, *143, 144, 145*

    and electricity, 18, 24, 25, 27, 53, 66

    and engineering, 18, 24, 25, 33, 71, 72, 76

    Great Waiting Room, *See* Pennsylvania Station (First), waiting hall

    Guastavino domes, *70*, 71, 72

    interior, 61, 62, *63*, 64–73, 77, 166–167

    ornamentation, 43, 58

    plan, 60, 61, 75, 81

    and real estate, 12, 17, 33, 34–37, 42, 82, 85–92, 95–96, 99–100, 153

    and redevelopment, 93–101

    site clearance, 34–38

    tunnels, 18, 22, 24, 25, 26, 27, 34, 77, 78, *131*

    and urbanism, 35–36, 81–83, 85, 102, 189

    waiting hall, *47, 48, 50, 52*, 60, 62, *63*, 64–67, 68, 72, 73, 74, 75, 76, 77, 82, 107, 115, *120, 121, 122, 123, 124, 125, 126, 127, 128, 130*, 166, *177*

Pennsylvania Station (New), 153–196

    building services, 174

    concourses, *172, 173*, 174, 181, *182*

    Intermodal Hall, 154, *155, 167*, 172, 175–176, *177, 179*, 181, 185, 186, *187*, 189, 190, 193; shell structure, 176, *177, 178, 179, 180, 181*, 186, *188*

    media wall, 181, *182*, 193

    Platform Area, 154, *182*

    redesign, 168–170, 171–174

    and retail, 175

    Train Room, 154, *155*, 174, 181, *182, 183, 184*, 185, 193

    and urbanism, 156, 158, 175, 189–192, 196

Pennsylvania Station Redevelopment Corporation (PSRC), 159, 160, 161

Pennsylvania Terminal Real Estate Company, 91

Pennsylvania Tunnel Extension and Terminal Project, 24

Percy Pyne Mansion, 103, 106

Philadelphia, Pa., 19, 21, 40, 94, 99, 100

Pittsburgh, Pa., 21

Platt, Geoffrey, 105, 106

Port Authority of New York and New Jersey, 102, 160

Port Authority Trans-Hudson, *See* PATH Corporation

Port Morris, Bronx, New York City, N.Y., 25

Port of New York, 11

Port of New York Authority, *See* Port Authority of New York and New Jersey

Power house, *39, 77*, 78, 90

Progressive Architecture, 102

Propylaea, Acropolis, Athens, Greece, *58*, 59

PSRC, *See* Pennsylvania Station Redevelopment Corporation

Queens, New York City, N.Y., 18, 24, 25

Queensboro Bridge, 23

Railway Age Gazette, 25

Rapid Transit Commission, 83; *See also* Board of Rapid Transit Commissioners

Rea, Samuel, 12, 21, 22, 24, 33, 35, 42, 64, 75, 76, 78, 79, 81, 82, 83, 85, 86, 87, 88, 89, 90, 91; 1892 report, 21–22, 24

Reed & Stem, 79, 80

Richardson, William Symmes, 43, 69, 70, 72, 74, 76, 87, 91

Ringwood State Park, Ringwood, N.J., 104

Robinson, Douglas, 37

Rome, *See* Ancient Rome

Rose, Aaron, 104, 111, 114, *123*, *126*

Rose, Billy, 96

Rudolph, Paul, 101

Saarinen, Aline, 101

Saunders, Stuart, 95

Schiphol USA, 160

Scientific American, 64

Senate Park Commission, 41, 59, 65

Skidmore, Owings & Merrill, 11, 159, 161, 162, 191, *192*

Soane, John, 59

Society for the Prevention of Crime, 35

SOM, S*ee* Skidmore, Owings & Merrill

Special Committee on New York Surplus Property, 88

St. Louis Exposition, *See* Louisiana Purchase Exposition (St. Louis, Mo., 1904)

St. Michael, Church of, New York City, N.Y., 37

St. Peter's, Rome, Italy, 64, 65; colonnade *58*, 59

Starrett, Paul, 51

Staten Island, New York City, N.Y., 22

Steele, Fritz, 35

Stern, Isaac, 103

Stillman, William, 59

Street cars, 33

Stubbins, Hugh, 102

Subway system (New York City), 17, 22, 33, 34, 74, 75, 82, 83, 91, 92, 93, 100, 155, 163, 167, 174, 191, 193, 196

Sunnyside, Queens, New York City, N.Y., 24, 25

Symes, James, 97, 98, 99, 100, 101

Tenderloin (neighborhood), Manhattan, New York City, N.Y., 35, 36, 37

Times Square, 33, 83, 163

Train sheds, 53, 66, 69

Transit Authority, *See* Metropolitan Transportation Authority, New York City Transit

Transportation Infrastructure Financing and Innovation Act (TIFIA), 160

Union Pacific Railroad, 94

Union Station, Washington, D.C., 41, 56, 65, 76

United Railroads of New Jersey, 19

United States Congress, 101

United States General Post Office (James A. Farley Building), *48*, *59*, *80*, *84*, 85, 86, 107, 112, *133*, *149*, 154–196; annex, 86, *155*, 165, 185, 187

United States Postal Service, 155, 158, 159, 160, 162, 166, 168, 170, 189

United States Supreme Court, 107

University Club, 41

Vanderbilt, William K., 79

Venturi, Robert, 102

Wagner, Robert, 105, 106

Wall Street, 17

Wall Street Journal, 42, 90, 99

Ware, William, 52

Warren and Wetmore, 80

Washington, D.C., 20, 21, 40, 41, 56, 94, 157, 192

Washington Square, 22
Webb & Knapp, 96
Weehawken, N.J., 24
Weinman, Adolf, 58
Westinghouse Church Kerr & Company, 70
Westside Competition, 190–191, *192*
White, Lawrence Grant, 54, 97
White, Norval, 102
White, Stanford, 54, *78*, 79, 97; murder of, 43
White House, 158
Wing, Wayman C., 111
World Trade Center, 17

Zeckendorf, William, 96, 97, 98, 101
Ziel, Ron, 104